Federal Deposit Insurance Corporation:

The First Fifty Years

A History of the FDIC
1933-1983

Federal Deposit Insurance Corporation
Washington, D.C.
1984

A commemorative stamp marking the 50th anniversary of the FDIC was unveiled as part of a reception program on June 15, 1983. Vice President George Bush, Postmaster General William Bolger, FDIC Chairman William Isaac and Mrs. Bush joined in the ceremony officially opening the anniversary observance.

Photo: Official White House Photograph

Prologue

On March 3 banking operations in the United States ceased. To review at this time the causes of this failure of our banking system is unnecessary. Suffice it to say that the government has been compelled to step in for the protection of depositors and the business of the nation.

As President Franklin D. Roosevelt spoke these words to Congress on March 9, 1933, the nation's troubled banking system lay dormant. More than 9,000 banks had ceased operations between the stock market crash in October 1929 and the banking holiday in March 1933. The economy was in the midst of the worst economic depression in modern history.

Out of the ruins, birth was given to the FDIC three months later when the President signed the Banking Act of 1933. Opposition to the measure had earlier been voiced by the President, the Chairman of the Senate Banking Committee and the American Bankers Association. They believed a system of deposit insurance would be unduly expensive and would unfairly subsidize poorly managed banks. Public opinion, however, was squarely behind a federal depositor protection plan.

By any standard, deposit insurance was an immediate success in restoring stability to the system. The bank failure rate dropped precipitously, with only nine insured banks failing during 1934. During the 30-year period beginning with World War II, the workings of the economy and the conservative behavior of bank regulators and the banking industry created a situation that posed few risks to the financial system, and the importance of deposit insurance in maintaining stability declined. Indeed, Wright Patman, the then-Chairman of the House banking committee, argued in a speech in 1963 that there were too few bank failures — that we had moved too far in the direction of bank safety.

While it is doubtful that a cause-and-effect relationship exists, Chairman Patman's wish has been realized. Banking has become a considerably more competitive business — more responsive to credit needs and more willing to assume greater risks in meeting those needs. While this development is very positive from the viewpoint of American consumers, farmers and businesses, banks have become concomitantly more vulnerable to changes in economic conditions.

Bank failures have increased in size and number in the past decade, culminating in a post-World War II record number of failures in the 1981-83 period. From the beginning of 1981 to date in 1983, the FDIC has handled 100 bank failures, including 18 of the 25 largest in FDIC history (the FDIC handled 6 failures on a single day in 1983, which was more than the number of failures in a typical year during the 1950s and 1960s). These 100 banks held assets of $24 billion compared to only $9 billion held by the 568 insured banks that failed prior to 1981. The FDIC's estimated losses during this three-year period amounted to $2.2 billion compared to less than $200 million on the previous 568 failures. The FDIC is currently involved in 170 active receiverships, is managing 65,000 receivership assets with an aggregate book value of $4.3 billion, and is a plaintiff or defendant in over 6,000 lawsuits related to receivership activities.

The insurance system has weathered the challenges presented by this staggering volume of activity. Public confidence in the banking system has been maintained without the expenditure of one penny of taxpayer money. The FDIC's insurance fund — whose revenues are derived from bank assessments and interest earned on investments in U.S. Treasury obligations — has grown rapidly from $11 billion at the beginning of 1981 to over $15 billion today.

The events of the past few years and the evolving process of deregulation have prompted the FDIC to reexamine the role of deposit insurance and to revise its attitudes and methods of operation. Our basic concern is that the existence of deposit insurance and, more importantly, the way in which the FDIC has handled most failed banks have provided too much comfort to larger depositors and other bank creditors. With a perception of minimal risk, there is little incentive for larger depositors to exert the degree of market discipline present in other industries. This situation has placed the deposit insurance agencies in a position where they must act in place of the market.

The trend away from market participation in the regulation of bank behavior probably dates from the founding of the FDIC. Over most of this period, when banks operated in a protected and stable environment, the substitution of regulatory for market discipline caused little concern. With the more recent move toward increasingly competitive banking markets, controlling bank risks through a formal regulatory mechanism is more complex and imposes substantial economic costs on both the industry and society as a whole. A better solution is to shift the regulatory balance toward a greater role for the market.

iv

This was the primary conclusion reached in a comprehensive study of the federal deposit insurance system completed and submitted to Congress by the FDIC in the spring of 1983. The means recommended to achieve this goal was to modify the way the FDIC handles bank failures to place uninsured depositors and other creditors at greater risk. As a supplement to this effort, it also was recommended that the FDIC vary deposit insurance premiums according to the risk a bank poses to the insurance fund and to charge for special supervisory activities. In November of 1983, the FDIC submitted to Congress proposed legislation to implement these changes.

The proposed legislation represents a vital first step in rationalizing the regulatory and insurance systems. The entire spectrum of other questions relating to the further deregulation of banking and the appropriate regulatory structure is currently under close study by Congress and various government agencies. For our part, we believe that providing adequate insurance coverage in an evenhanded manner should be the FDIC's principal role. We do not believe the FDIC should divert its resources to the examination of banks that pose little risk to the deposit insurance fund, or to other activities not directly related to our insurance function. This is the direction in which the FDIC is moving.

While this history was prepared by FDIC staff, a genuine attempt has been made to treat objectively the role of the FDIC during the first 50 years of its existence. This is important not only from the standpoint of intellectual honesty, but because this piece is intended to improve understanding of the FDIC and the issues to be considered by those responsible for reforming the system.

We hope the need for deposit insurance will never again be so great as it was in the 1930s. Nevertheless, as the FDIC embarks on its second half-century, the challenges at hand are greater than at any time in the past four decades.

William M. Isaac
Chairman
Federal Deposit Insurance Corporation
December 21, 1983

cAcknowledgments

This history was prepared by the Division of Research and Strategic Planning, with main contributions from Detta Voesar and James McFadyen. Other contributors were Stanley C. Silverberg, Director of the division, who also directed the project, and William R. Watson, Associate Director. Jean Roane, Alane Lehfeld and the Library staff provided valuable research assistance. Cathy Curtis supplied greatly appreciated secretarial services throughout the numerous drafts.

Steven A. Seelig of the Division of Liquidation was particularly helpful in the early stages of the project. Useful comments, suggestions and information were provided by many people in various FDIC offices, among whom were William M. Dudley, Division of Liquidation; Donald L. Pfeiffer, Jr. and Ken A. Quincy, Division of Bank Supervision; Douglas Birdzell, Joseph A. DiNuzzo, Roger A. Hood and Carroll R. Shifflett, Legal Division; and Ronald E. Doherty, Division of Accounting and Corporate Services. Carter Golembe of Golembe Associates, Inc., also reviewed the manuscript.

Former employees Neil Greensides and John Early, both of whom are past directors of the Division of Bank Supervision, granted interviews which provided valuable personal insights into past events and personalities.

Gratitude is also due Geoffrey Wade, Geri Pavey and others in the Graphics and Printing Unit.

Table
of
Contents

Chapter 1
Introduction

The Federal Deposit Insurance Corporation has served as an integral part of the nation's financial system for 50 years. Established by the Banking Act of 1933 at the depth of the most severe banking crisis in the nation's history, its immediate contribution was the restoration of public confidence in banks. While the agency has grown and modified its operations in response to changing economic conditions and shifts in the banking environment, the mission of the FDIC over the past five decades has remained unchanged: to insure bank deposits and reduce the economic disruptions caused by bank failures.

Background

At the time of its adoption in 1933, deposit insurance had a record of experiments at the state level extending back to 1829. New York was the first of 14 states that adopted plans, over a period from 1829 to 1917, to insure or guarantee bank deposits or other obligations that served as currency. The purposes of the various state insurance plans were similar: to protect communities from the economic disruptions caused by bank failures; and to protect depositors against losses. In the majority of cases the insurance plans eventually proved unworkable. By early 1930, the last of these plans had ceased operations.

At the federal level, deposit insurance had a legislative history reaching back to 1886. A total of 150 proposals for deposit insurance or guaranty were made in Congress between 1886 and 1933. Many of these proposals were prompted by financial crises, though none was as severe as the crisis that developed in the early 1930s. The events of that period finally convinced the general public that measures of a national scope were needed to alleviate the disruptions caused by bank failures.

From the stock market crash in the fall of 1929 to the end of 1933, about 9,000 banks suspended operations, resulting in losses to depositors of about $1.3 billion. The closure of 4,000 banks in the first few months of 1933, and the panic that accompanied these suspensions, led President Roosevelt to declare a bank holiday on March 6, 1933. The financial system was on the verge of collapse, and both the manufacturing and agricultural sectors were operating at a fraction of capacity.

The crisis environment led to the call for deposit insurance. Ultimately, the force of public opinion spurred Congress to enact deposit insurance legislation. The Banking Act of 1933, which created the FDIC, was signed by President Roosevelt on June 16, 1933.

By almost any measure, the FDIC has been successful in maintaining public confidence in the banking system. Prior to the establishment of the FDIC, large-scale cash demands of fearful depositors were often the fatal blow to banks that otherwise might have survived. Widespread bank runs have become a thing of the past and no longer constitute a threat to the industry. The money supply both on a local and national level has ceased to be subject to contractions caused by bank failures. The liquidation of failed bank assets no longer disrupts local or national markets and a significant portion of a community's assets are no longer tied up in bankruptcy proceedings when a bank fails.

The Early Years

The history of the FDIC cannot be considered apart from changes in economic and banking conditions. The early years of the FDIC's existence were not a period of risk taking by banks. Caution marked the attitudes of both the supervisory agencies and the industry itself. For their part, the supervisory agencies viewed the events that culminated in the nationwide bank holiday as a banking rather than a monetary phenomenon. The prevailing philosophy was that unfettered competition in the past had resulted in excesses and abuses in banking. Consequently, the supervisory agencies followed what the FDIC later termed as a policy of keeping banks and banking practices within the bounds of rightful competition.

The attitude of bankers was similarly circumspect. Those who survived the Depression were chastened by that experience. The effect of the Depression experience on the industry was reflected in the subsequent massive liquidity buildup undertaken by banks. By 1937, for example, cash and holdings of U.S. government securities comprised about 52 percent of the industry's total assets, or more than twice the proportion held in 1929. To the dismay of would-be borrowers, banks continued to stress liquidity for many more years.

Legislation enacted in the 1930s to insulate banks from competing with one another too aggressively also restrained bank behavior. The Banking Act of 1933 outlawed the payment

4

of interest by member banks on demand deposits. The Act also authorized the Federal Reserve Board to set a ceiling on time deposit rates offered by member banks in order to forestall ruinous competition among banks. In addition, the 1933 law ordered the separation of investment from commercial banking to be completed by mid-June 1934.

The Banking Act of 1935 similarly incorporated provisions designed to limit bank behavior. The Act expanded the FDIC's supervisory powers and set more rigorous standards for admission to insurance. The 1935 law required the FDIC to prohibit the payment of interest on demand deposits in insured nonmember banks and to limit the rates of interest paid.

While the effects of a still-depressed economy also engendered caution on the part of bankers and regulators, conditions improved from the low point reached in 1933. Unemployment declined significantly, real GNP increased at an average annual compound growth rate of 9.5 percent between 1933 and 1937, and price increases were moderate. The recession of 1937-1938 interrupted this pattern of economic expansion. Owing to the continuous improvement in the banking system that had occurred since the banking holiday of 1933, however, banks were able to meet without difficulty the strains resulting from the decline in business activity that ensued. Following the recession, economic conditions improved once again as real GNP rose and unemployment declined.

The FDIC handled 370 bank failures from 1934 through 1941. Most of these were small banks. Without the presence of federal deposit insurance, the number of bank failures undoubtedly would have been greater and the bank population would have been reduced. The presence of deposit insurance also may have limited the necessity for some banks to merge, and may have indirectly encouraged retention of restrictive state branching laws.

The end of 1941 marked the completion of eight years of successful operation of the system of federal insurance of bank deposits. It also marked the close of a period of economic recovery under peacetime conditions, which provided especially favorable circumstances for the establishment of deposit insurance and for improvement in the financial condition of banks.

The Period 1942-1972

During World War II, government financial policies and private sector restrictions produced an expanding banking system. Total bank assets at the end of 1945 were nearly double the $91 billion total at the end of 1941. Large-scale war financing of the federal government was the primary factor contributing to the rise in bank assets. Banks played a major role in financing the war effort by lending to other bond buyers, by handling the bulk of the war loan campaign sales volume, and by purchasing government obligations themselves. At the end of 1945, holdings of those obligations accounted for 57 percent of total bank assets.

Loan losses were practically nonexistent during the war years and bank failures declined significantly. Only 28 insured banks failed in the period 1942-1945. The decline in the number of troubled banks can be ascribed primarily to the highly liquid state of bank assets, the absence of deposit outflows, and vigorous business activity.

As the war drew to a close and ended, the transfer to peacetime conditions raised questions whether the economy would enter another depression or experience disruptive inflation. Many individuals feared that unemployment, declining income and business failures would ensue. However, inflation rather than deflation ensued. The public had a large volume of liquid assets, there was a tremendous demand for goods, and the immediate problem was one of inadequate production rather than of unemployment.

The banking industry was in a favorable position to finance the spending spree that was poised to occur. Banks had emerged from World War II in very liquid condition. Yet, many individuals expressed doubts whether banks were up to the task of resuming their traditional lending function.

These concerns proved groundless. In 1947 alone, bank lending increased from 16 percent to 25 percent of the industry's assets. Lending subsequently reached 40 percent of assets in the mid-1950s, and 50 percent in the early 1960s.

This resurgence of lending did not produce a concomitant increase in loan losses. Several factors accounted for the relatively low level of loan losses during the postwar years. First, banking behavior by present standards continued to be very conservative. In addition, the economy remained strong. Recessions were reasonably mild and short. This was a period of

6

general prosperity, with a secularly increasing real GNP and relatively low unemployment.

Conservative banking practices and favorable economic conditions resulted in few bank failures during the late 1940s and 1950s. However, the low incidence of failures was regarded by some as a sign that the bank regulators were overly strict. In a speech marking the dedication of the headquarters building of the FDIC in 1963, Wright Patman, then-Chairman of the House Banking and Currency Committee, declared:

> . . . I think we should have more bank failures. The record of the last several years of almost no bank failures and, finally last year, no bank failure at all, is to me a danger signal that we have gone too far in the direction of bank safety.

Until about 1960, banks continued to operate in a safe, insulated environment. Then banks gradually began to change the way they operated. The Depression experience ceased to be a dominant influence on bank management. The new generation of bankers who came to power in the 1960s abandoned the traditional conservatism that had characterized the industry for many years. Instead, they began to strive for more rapid growth in assets, deposits and income.

The trend toward aggressiveness and risk taking was particularly pronounced among large banks. These banks also began pressing at the boundaries of allowable activities. They expanded into fields considered by some to involve more than the traditional degree of risk for commercial banks.

There were other changes during the 1960s that had an impact on banking. States began to liberalize branching laws. The bank holding company vehicle was developed as an alternative form of multi-office banking and as a means to enter new product markets. With the introduction of the large negotiable certificate of deposit, banks' reliance on purchased money increased. In addition to the bank regulatory agencies having to monitor these developments, federal legislation gave them additional enforcement responsibilities in the areas of securities disclosure, antitrust and consumer protection.

Until the mid-1970s, banks were not noticeably harmed by the movement toward increased risk taking. Generally favorable economic conditions enabled many otherwise marginal borrowers to meet their obligations. With the exception of relatively mild recessions, the economy produced high levels of production, employment and income during most of the period.

7

The Period 1973 — Present

Bank behavior has continued to undergo significant changes during the past ten years. Bank reliance on purchased money has increased, even for moderate-sized banks. Demand balances have become less important and, in the case of the household sector, most of these now pay interest. Cheap deposits, in general, have become scarce. Banks have entered new product markets, geographic expansion possibilities have broadened and traditional banking services are now being offered by financial and commercial conglomerates. While these changes have enabled banks to remain competitive, particular aspects of bank behavior, such as the growing dependence on purchased money, have made the industry more vulnerable to adverse economic conditions.

The performance of the economy over the past 10 years has not been very strong. The first of two major recessions during the decade occurred in 1973-1975. The severity of the recession contributed to a substantial increase in commercial bank loan losses and an increase in both the number of problem banks and bank failures. It was during this period that the FDIC encountered the first large bank failures. The 1973-1975 recession led to substantial real estate loan problems. In many instances these persisted well beyond the onset of economic recovery and, as a result, the bank failure rate remained comparatively high, peaking in 1976 at 16, the highest number since 1940.

The mid-1970s also were characterized by other special problems. Repercussions were felt throughout the economy as a result of the rapid increase in oil prices that began in 1973, and the subsequent role of U.S. banks in recycling petrodollars. The oil price shock contributed to a rising inflation rate and new highs in interest rates in 1974.

While the banking industry did not fully recover from the effects of the recession until 1977, the following year brought renewed pressures on the industry. In 1978, interest rates on securities markedly surpassed the rates payable by depository institutions for savings and time accounts. Deposit growth slowed, particularly at thrifts, as alternative investment instruments and yields became relatively attractive.

In 1979 and early 1980, inflation burst upward, along with interest rates. The rise in interest rates was spurred not only by inflationary pressures, but also by a change in Federal Reserve monetary policy in October 1979. The resultant high interest

8

rates, in combination with an unduly heavy emphasis on fixed-rate, long-term lending, caused severe problems for the thrift industry.

In addition to the stresses produced by high interest rates, financial institutions had to cope with the changes engendered by the passage of banking deregulation legislation in 1980. The Depository Institutions Deregulation and Monetary Control Act, the most sweeping banking reform package enacted since 1933, mandated the elimination of interest rate ceilings by 1986. Other provisions of the Act liberalized lending powers of federal thrifts and preempted some state usury laws. Two years later, in 1982, Congress passed the Garn-St Germain Depository Institutions Act, which took deregulation even further and gave the regulators more flexibility in dealing with failing institutions.

A severe recession in 1981-1982 placed further strains on the banking industry. The recession arrived at a time when bankers were willing (and may even have felt forced) to take additional risks in order to maintain interest margins in the face of rising liability costs. The lure of lending to growth industries had led some banks to excessive loan concentrations in fragile industries. An oil surplus and the resultant decline in prices, for example, caught many bankers who had invested heavily in independent oil and gas development companies that suddenly were no longer viable.

Recession-related factors, in combination with high and volatile interest rates and deregulation, caused loan charge-offs to increase by more than 50 percent in 1982 alone. The number of problem banks also increased sharply. In 1982, the number of bank failures hit 42, a new post-World War II high. Moreover, despite the turnaround in the economy during the first half of 1983, there were 27 commercial bank failures during this period.

These developments have had a major impact on the FDIC. There is a greater sense of bank exposure and risk of failure that exists not just among those who regulate and follow banks, but among the general public as well. The FDIC has had to adjust its bank supervision practices, as well as dramatically increase its liquidation work force. Changes in the complexity and size of the banking industry over the past decade have presented the FDIC with challenges and problems as formidable as those faced by the FDIC during its first decade.

This book chronicles the history of the FDIC during its first 50 years. Chapter 2 focuses on the antecedents to federal deposit insurance. The events that led to the passage of the Banking Acts of 1933 and 1935 are discussed in Chapter 3. The financial and internal operations of the FDIC are detailed in Chapter 4. Inasmuch as the handling of failures and bank supervision have encompassed the FDIC's primary areas of responsibility, each of these areas is covered separately in Chapters 5 and 6, respectively. Some final thoughts on the occasion of the FDIC's 50th anniversary are offered in the Epilogue.

On June 16, 1933, President Franklin Roosevelt signed the Banking Act of 1933, a part of which established the FDIC. At Roosevelt's immediate right and left were Sen. Carter Glass of Virginia and Rep. Henry Steagall of Alabama, the two most prominent figures in the bill's development.

Photo: Wide World Photos

11

Chapter 2
Antecedents
of the
FDIC

Insurance of Bank Obligations, 1829-1866

During the years immediately following the organization of the federal government in 1789, banks were chartered by special acts of state legislatures or the Congress, usually for a limited number of years. Initially, bank failures were nonexistent. It was not until 1809, with the failure of the Farmers Bank of Gloucester, Rhode Island, that people realized that such an event was even possible.[1] Any notion that this failure represented an isolated incident was dispelled after the first wave of bank failures occurred five years later. The ensuing economic disruptions caused by these and subsequent bank failures fueled demands for banking reform.

In 1829, New York became the first state to adopt a bank-obligation insurance program.[2] New York's program was devised by Joshua Forman, a Syracuse businessman. The insurance concept embodied in his plan was suggested by the regulations of the Hong merchants in Canton.[3] The regulations required merchants who held special charters to trade with foreigners to be liable for one another's debts. Writing in 1829, when bank-supplied circulating medium was largely in the form of bank notes rather than deposits, Forman noted:

> The case of our banks is very similar; they enjoy in common the exclusive right of making a paper currency for the people of the state, and by the same rule should in common be answerable for that paper.[4]

---

[1]Carter H. Golembe, "Origins of Deposit Insurance in the Middle West, 1834-1866," *The Indiana Magazine of History*, Vol. LI, June, 1955, No. 2, p. 113.

[2]The term "bank obligation" refers to both circulating notes and deposits.

[3]*Assembly Journal*, New York State, 1829, p. 179.

[4]Ibid., p. 179.

The plan conceived by Forman had three principal components:

- The establishment of an insurance fund, to which all banks had to pay an assessment;

- A board of commissioners, which was granted bank examination powers; and

- A specified list of investments for bank capital.

The first two provisions were adopted virtually intact; the proposal pertaining to the investment of bank capital initially was rejected. Upon reconsideration during the 1830s, the bank capital proposal was modified and subsequently enacted.

Between 1831-1858, five additional states adopted insurance programs: Vermont, Indiana, Michigan, Ohio, and Iowa. The purposes of the various plans were similar: (1) to protect communities from severe fluctuations of the circulating medium caused by bank failures; and (2) to protect individual depositors and noteholders against losses. Available evidence indicates that the first of these, concern with the restoration of the circulating medium *per se*, predominated.[5]

Nature of plans. In striving to meet these insurance goals, the states employed one of three approaches. Following New York's lead, Vermont and Michigan established insurance funds. Indiana did not; instead, all participating banks were required mutually to guarantee the liabilities of a failed bank. The insurance programs adopted by Ohio and Iowa incorporated both approaches. While participating banks were bound together by a mutual guaranty provision, an insurance fund was available to reimburse the banks in the event special assessments were necessary immediately to pay creditors of failed banks. The insurance fund was replenished from liquidation proceeds.

Table 2-1 summarizes the principal provisions of the six programs which operated between 1829-1866.

Coverage. In the first four programs adopted, insurance coverage primarily extended to circulating notes and deposits. New York later restricted coverage to circulating notes. In the case of Ohio and Iowa, insurance coverage from the outset only extended to circulating notes. None of the six programs placed a dollar limit on the amount of insurance provided an individual bank creditor.

---

[5]Carter H. Golembe, "The Deposit Insurance Legislation of 1933: An Examination of Its Antecedents and Its Purposes," *Political Science Quarterly*, Vol. LXXV, No. 2, June, 1960, p. 189.

The extension of insurance coverage to bank notes in all of the six programs reflected their importance as a circulating medium. Because it was common practice for banks to extend credit by using bank notes, nearly one-half of the circulating medium prior to 1860 was in this form. In those states that limited insurance coverage to bank notes, the belief was that banks affected the circulating medium only through their issuance. Additionally, it was believed that depositors could select their banks, whereas noteholders had considerably less discretion and thus were in greater need of protection.[6]

Methods used to protect creditors of banks in financial difficulty. Ad hoc measures frequently were taken in some of the six states to protect creditors of banks in financial difficulty. Faced with the possible insolvency of several banks in 1837, New York State's Comptroller began redeeming their notes from the insurance fund. This action prevented the banks from failing and they eventually were able to reimburse the insurance fund. In 1842, New York faced a more serious crisis after the failure of eleven participating banks within a three-year period threatened the solvency of the insurance fund. The legislature authorized the State Comptroller to sell bonds sufficient to meet all claims against the insurance fund. The bonds later were redeemed from subsequent payments into the fund by participating banks.

Other states similarly grappled with the question of whether to assist or close a distressed bank. On several occasions authorities in Ohio kept a number of distressed banks from closing by levying special assessments upon healthy participating banks. Indiana and Iowa also granted financial assistance to distressed banks.

Method of paying creditors of failed banks. Only the programs of Ohio and Iowa provided for immediate payment of insured obligations. Necessary funds were made available in those two states through special assessments levied on the sound participating banks. Creditors in New York, Vermont and Michigan were not paid until the liquidation of a failed bank had been completed. Indiana's program provided that creditors were to be paid within one year after a bank failed if liquidation proceeds and stockholder contributions were insufficient to cover realized losses.

Role of bank supervision. Bank supervision was an essential element of the insurance programs that operated prior to 1866.

---

[6]Federal Deposit Insurance Corporation, *Annual Report,* 1952 (1953), p. 61.

15

Table 2-1. Principal Provisions of Bank-Obligation Insurance Programs In Operation 1829 - 1866

State	Period of operation[1]	Obligations Insured	Banks participating	Assessments; size of fund	Payment of bank creditors
New York	1829-1866	1829-42, all debts[2] 1842-66, circulating notes[3]	All banks established or rechartered subsequent to passage of act[4]	Annually ½ of 1% of capital stock to maximum of 3%. If fund reduced, annual assessment not to exceed above rate until fund restored to maximum.	After completion of liquidation of failed bank.
Vermont	1831-1866	All debts[2]	All banks established or rechartered subsequent to passage of act[5]	Annually ¾ of 1% of capital stock to maximum of 4½%. If fund reduced, annual assessments not to exceed above rate until fund restored to maximum.	After completion of liquidation of failed bank.
Indiana	1834-1866	All debts[2]	Branch Banks[6]	No specific amount; special assessments as necessary.	Within one year after failure, if liquidation proceeds and stockholder contributions insufficient.
Michigan	1836-1842	All debts[2]	All banks established or rechartered subsequent to passage of act	Annually ½ of 1% of capital stock to maximum of 3%. If fund reduced, annual assessments not to exceed above rate until fund restored to maximum.	After completion of liquidation of failed bank.
Ohio	1845-1866	Circulating notes	Branch Banks	Single assessment prior to opening of bank: 10% of amount of circulating notes. Thereafter assessments at above rate applicable only to additional circulating notes, if any, issued by bank.	Immediately, through special assessments on solvent Branch Banks. Assessments to be repaid from insurance fund, and fund repaid from proceeds of liquidation of assets of failed bank.

16

| Iowa | 1858-1865 | Circulating notes | Branch Banks | Single assessment prior to opening of bank: 12½% of amount of circulating notes. Thereafter assessments at above rate applicable only to additional circulating notes, if any, issued by bank. | Immediately, through special assessments on solvent Branch Banks. Assessments to be repaid from insurance fund and fund repaid from proceeds of liquidation of assets of failed bank. |

---

[1] In a number of cases the law was repealed subsequent to the terminal date shown above. In some of the first six States closing dates may have preceded date shown by one year.

[2] Included circulating notes, deposits, and miscellaneous liabilities; excluded capital accounts.

[3] Act of April 12, 1842.

[4] Free Banks, which were authorized in 1838, did not participate in insurance.

[5] Free banks, which were authorized in 1851, did not participate in insurance. In 1842 participating banks were authorized under specified conditions to withdraw from insurance.

[6] Branch Banks were essentially independent banks which possessed their own officers, distributed earnings to their own stockholders, and which collectively constituted the "State Bank" in these States.

Source: Federal Deposit Insurance Corporation, *Annual Report, 1952* (1953). pp. 62-63.

17

Worried depositors gather outside a failed New York City banking house in the late 1800s.

Photo: Reprinted by permission from *The Bankers Magazine,* Volume 152, Number 1, Winter 1969. Copyright 1969, Warren, Gorham & Lamont, Inc., 210 South Street, Boston, Mass. All Rights Reserved.

18

The function of supervision was essentially twofold: (1) to reduce the potential risk exposure of the various insurance programs; and (2) to provide some measure of assurance to well managed banks that the unsound banking practices of badly managed banks would not go completely unchecked.[7] Table 2-2 summarizes the principal provisions relating to bank supervision in the six insurance states.

Better supervision of banks was achieved by the programs with mutual guaranty than by the simple insurance fund programs.[8] Under the mutual guaranty programs in Indiana, Ohio and Iowa, supervisory officials were largely selected by, and accountable to, the participating banks. The officials were given wide latitude to check unsound banking practices because the participating banks were keenly aware that the cost of lax supervision ultimately would be borne by them.

During the Indiana program's 30 years of operation, not one state-chartered bank failed. Indiana's success principally was attributable to the quality of bank supervision.[9] A strong supervisory board was the cornerstone of the program. The board, which included four members appointed by the Indiana General Assembly and one representative from each of the participating banks, could close any member bank. The causes for closing a bank were: (1) insolvency; (2) mismanagement; and (3) refusal to comply with any legal directive of the board. The board's power was absolute since there was no provision for appeal to the courts or to any other state agency.

Supervisory authorities in Ohio and Iowa could issue cease-and-desist orders, as well as require banks to be closed. Ohio had four banks fail: one in 1852 because of defalcation and three in 1854 because of asset deterioration. While none failed in Iowa, it should be noted that Iowa's program operated during a period of more favorable economic conditions.

Assessments and the insurance funds. Insurance fund assessments were levied on capital stock or insured obligations. To provide a basis for comparison with later assessment rates under federal deposit insurance, previous researchers have computed the equivalent average annual rate on total obligations

---

[7]Carter H. Golembe and Clark Warburton, *Insurance of Bank Obligations in Six States* (Washington, D.C.: Federal Deposit Insurance Corporation, 1958), pp. I-9 - I-10.

[8]Federal Deposit Insurance Corporation, *Annual Report*, 1953 (1954), p. 59.

[9]Golembe and Warburton, p. I-18.

Table 2-2. Principal Provisions Relating to Supervision of Banks Participating in Bank-Obligation Insurance Systems, Six States, 1829-1866

State	Supervisory agency	Bank examination	Condition reports	Enforcement powers of supervisory officials
New York	1829-37. Three Bank Commissioners; one appointed by Governor; two by banks. 1837-43. Three Bank Commissioners appointed by Governor. 1843-51. State Comptroller. 1851-66. Banking Department; superintendent appointed by Governor.	1829-43. Each bank three times per year; additional examinations if requested by three participating banks. 1843-66. Examination only when bank was believed to be insolvent or to have submitted false condition report.	1829-43. Annually to Bank Commissioners. 1843-66. Quarterly to Comptroller; Superintendent of Banking Department. Content expanded.	If bank insolvent or had violated law could apply to court of chancery for injunction against continued operation.
Vermont	1831-37. Three Bank Commissioners; one appointed by legislature; two by banks. 1837-58. One Bank Commissioner appointed by legislature.	Each bank once per year; additional examinations if requested by a stockholder or bank debtor.	Annually to Bank Commissioners.	If bank insolvent or had violated law could apply to court of chancery for injunction against continued operation.
Indiana	1834-55. Board of Directors of the State Bank of Indiana; President and four directors appointed by legislature; one director by each Branch Bank. 1856-65. Board of Directors of the Bank of the State of Indiana; four directors appointed by legislature; one director by each Branch Bank; president by Board.	Each bank twice per year; additional examinations if requested by directors of a bank.	Monthly to Board.	If bank insolvent, had violated law, or was mismanaging its affairs could close bank. Could regulate dividend payments.[1] Could establish ratio of loans and discounts to capital for any or all banks between specified limits. Loan of deposited funds exempted.

Michigan	1836-37. One Bank Commissioner appointed by Governor. 1837-40. Three Bank Commissioners appointed by Governor. 1840-42. Attorney General.	1836-40. Each bank three times per year; additional examinations if requested by three participating banks. 1840-42. At Governor's request.	Annual to Bank Commissioners; Attorney General.	If bank insolvent or had violated law could apply to court of chancery for injunction against continued operation.
Ohio	Board of Control of the State Bank of Ohio; one member appointed by each Branch Bank; president by Board from outside its membership.	Left to discretion of Board; policy was to examine each bank once per year.	Quarterly to Board, policy to require monthly reports to Board.	If bank insolvent, had violated law, or any order of Board, could close bank. Could order any bank to reduce its circulation or liabilities to whatever level was deemed safe. Could determine proportion of reserve to be in vault cash.[1]
Iowa	Board of Directors of the State Bank of Iowa; three directors appointed by legislature; one director by each Branch Bank; president by Board.	Left to discretion of Board; policy was to examine each bank twice per year.	Monthly to Board.	If bank insolvent, had violated law, or any order of Board, could close bank. Could regulate dividend payments. Could order any bank to reduce its circulation or liabilities to whatever level was deemed safe.

[1] Not stipulated in law but assumed by agency.

Source: Carter H. Golembe and Clark Warburton, *Insurance of Bank Obligations in Six States* (Washington, D.C.: The Federal Deposit Insurance Corporation, 1958), pp. I-8, I-9.

(*i.e.*, deposits plus circulating notes) levied by the five states that had insurance funds (Table 2-3). On this basis, Michigan's annual rate of one-tenth of one percent most closely approximated the present statutory rate of one-twelfth of one percent under federal deposit insurance (before credits). Other rates were substantially higher, ranging from one-fifth of one percent in Vermont to almost two percent in Iowa.

Three insurance programs had positive fund balances at the time of their closing (Table 2-3). The Vermont and Michigan insurance funds were deficient by $22,000 and $1.2 million, respectively. In both states the first failures occurred before the insurance funds were adequately capitalized. Michigan's program collapsed under the strain. Although Vermont's fund subsequently recovered, it had a negative balance at the time the program closed due to the payment of unauthorized refunds to banks previously withdrawing from the program.

Demise of the insurance programs. Two primary factors contributed to the eventual collapse of the state insurance systems. The first factor was the emergence of the "free banking" movement in the 1830s. This movement developed in response to the void created by the closing of the Second Bank of the United States in 1836. To fill this void, many states enacted laws designed to ease bank entry restrictions. The movement produced an alternative for insurance of bank notes, which permitted a bank to post bonds and mortgages with state officials in an amount equal to its outstanding bank notes. Banks taking advantage of this alternative were excluded from insurance.[10] As the number of "free banks" increased, participation in state insurance programs declined. Consequently, the original intent to include all banks in the individual state insurance programs was thwarted.

The second factor was the establishment of the national bank system in 1863. In 1865, Congress levied a prohibitive tax on state bank notes causing many state-chartered banks to convert to national charters in order to escape the tax. As conversions increased, membership in the state insurance systems declined, eventually to the point where these programs ceased to exist.

Guaranty of Circulating Bank Notes by the Federal Government

National bank notes were collateralized by United States bonds. More importantly, the primary guaranty for the notes was the

---

[10]This exclusion did not apply in Michigan.

Table 2-3. Insurance Funds and Assessments, States with Bank-Obligation Insurance Systems, 1829-1866[1] ($ Thousands)

	New York (1829-1866)	Vermont (1831-1866)	Michigan (1836-1842)	Ohio (1845-1866)	Iowa (1858-1865)
Insurance funds:					
Average size	$192	$19	$0.3	$759	$196
As percent of—					
Average total obligations	0.6%	2.0%	.09%	7.7%	8.4%
Average insured obligations	1.0%	2.0%	.09%	11.5%	21.4%
Balance or deficiency at close of system	$13	−$22	−$1,198	$815[2]	$338[2]
Assessments and income available for insurance operations:	$3,221	$63	$3	$1,567	$338
Assessments paid[3]	3,120	63	3	1,567	338
Interest received[4]	101	.....	.....	.....	.....
Used for insurance operations	3,208	44	.....	722[5]	.....
Refunded to banks or State[6]	13	19	.....	845	338
Assessments necessary to cover insurance costs	$3,208	$66	$1,198	722[5]	.....
Equivalent average annual rate of assessments on total obligations:					
Paid	0.24%	0.2%	0.1%	0.8%	1.8%

[1] In Indiana the insurance system was one of mutual guaranty with no fund.
[2] Amount in fund in last year of full operation of insurance system.
[3] Assessments paid and used for insurance operations other than administrative expenses except in Michigan, where amount paid was completely absorbed by such expenses.
[4] In excess of amounts used to pay administrative expenses and amounts paid to banks. In Vermont, Ohio, and Iowa such expenses absorbed the whole of investment income.
[5] Total of special assessments used to redeem notes of failed banks or aid operating banks plus estimated amounts secured from assets in insurance funds of failed banks. Recoveries from other assets of such banks by insurance system are not known.
[6] In New York paid into State treasury; in Vermont refunded to six banks withdrawing prior to close of system; in Ohio refunded to one bank withdrawing prior to close of system and to all banks at close of system; in Iowa refunded to all banks at close of system.

Source: Federal Deposit Insurance Corporation, *Annual Report,* 1953 (1954), p. 56.

credit of the federal government rather than the value of the posted collateral. Holders of notes of a failed national bank were to be paid immediately and in full by the United States Treasury regardless of the value of the bonds backing the notes. As the Comptroller of the Currency stated in his first report to Congress:

> If the banks fail, and the bonds of the government are depressed in the market, the notes of the national banks must still be redeemed in full at the treasury of the United States. The holder has not only the public securities, but the faith of the nation pledged for their redemption.[11]

So long as national bank notes retained their relative importance in the circulating medium, bank-obligation insurance was considered unnecessary. However, bank deposits soon overtook and then eclipsed national bank notes in importance. By 1870, deposits were about twice, and by the end of the century seven times, circulating notes. It was against this backdrop that efforts were renewed to provide for deposit insurance. Various proposals to that effect were introduced at the federal and state levels. Although the first attempts were made in Congress as early as 1886, the states took the lead.

State Insurance of Bank Deposits, 1908-1930

Between 1907-1917, eight states adopted deposit insurance programs. Seven of the eight states were located west of the Mississippi in predominantly agricultural areas. Table 2-4 summarizes the principal provisions of the eight programs.

Coverage. Insurance coverage in the eight states only extended to deposits. Although the insurance programs were commonly known as "deposit guaranty" programs, the guaranty was that of a fund derived from assessments on the participating banks. In no instance did the state explicitly guarantee the deposits.

None of the states, except Kansas for a brief period, placed an insurance limit on the size of account or amount of deposits owned by a depositor. However, some restrictions were applied to various classes of deposits.

Methods of paying depositors of failed banks. In Kansas and Mississippi the depositors of a failed bank received interest-bearing certificates. Dividends on these certificates were paid from liquidation proceeds. Upon final liquidation of all assets, the balance due on the certificates was paid from the insurance fund.

---

[11]U.S., Comptroller of the Currency, *Annual Report*, November 28, 1863 (1864), p. 58.

Table 2-4.   Principal Provisions of Deposit Insurance Programs Adopted by Eight States, 1907-1917

State	Deposits insured	Banks participating[1]	Assessment on insured deposits[2]	Payment of depositors
Oklahoma Act of 1908[3] as amended or modified 1909, 1911, 1913	All deposits not otherwise secured and on which rate of interest was within limits specified by law.	Compulsory for all State banks and trust companies.	Annually ⅕ of 1% until fund equaled 2% of base. If fund reduced, special assessments at same rate annually.[4]	In cash by Bank Commission immediately upon taking possession of bank. If fund insufficient, in 6 percent certificates of indebtedness to be paid in order of issue. After 1913 certificates sold at not less than par for purpose of securing cash for depositors.
Kansas Act of 1909 as amended or modified 1911, 1921, 1923	All deposits not otherwise secured and on which rate of interest was within limits specified by law.	Voluntary for all incorporated State banks. Trust companies and private banks excluded. Banks organized after passage of Act eligible to apply after operating one year.	Annually ¹⁄₂₀ of 1% of base less capital and surplus until fund equaled $1 million. If fund reduced below $500,000 special assessment for amount necessary.	In interest-bearing certificates of indebtedness, reduced as proceeds of liquidation become available. Deficiency, if any, paid from fund.
Nebraska Act of 1909 as amended or modified 1911	All deposits except money deposited on a collateral agreement or condition other than an agreement for length of time to maturity and rate of interest.	Compulsory for all incorporated State banks.	Semi-annually ¹⁄₂₀ of 1% until fund equaled 1½% of base. If fund reduced below 1% assessment renewed and special assessments if necessary not to exceed 1% of base in any one year.	In cash from fund immediately after determination by the court of amount due depositors less cash immediately available to the receiver for such payments.

25

State	Deposits insured	Banks participating[1]	Assessment on insured deposits[2]	Payment of depositors
Texas Act of 1909 as amended or modified 1921, 1923	Non-interest-bearing deposits not otherwise secured. Excluded public deposits, secured deposits, certificates of deposit, deposits made for the purpose of converting a loan into a deposit covered by the fund, certificates of deposit converted to non-interest-bearing deposits within 90 days of failure.	All State-chartered banks required to choose between guaranty fund system or bond security system.	Annually ¼ of 1% of base until fund equalled $5 million. If fund reduced below $2 million, or below level of preceding January 1, special assessments not to exceed 2%.	In cash immediately, out of cash in failed banks and fund.
Mississippi Act of 1914	All deposits not otherwise secured nor bearing interest exceeding 4% per annum.	Voluntary until May 15, 1915. Thereafter compulsory for all banks operating under State law including trust companies and savings banks.	Annually ¹⁄₂₀ of 1% of average guaranteed deposits, less capital and surplus until fund approximated $500,000 over and above initial contribution. If fund depleted, special assessments at same rate not to exceed five in any one year.	In interest-bearing certificates of indebtedness, reduced as proceeds of liquidation become available. Deficiency, if any, paid from fund.
South Dakota Act of 1915 as amended or modified 1921	All deposits not otherwise secured. Deposits could not pay interest in excess of 5% unless authorized by depositors guaranty fund commission and in no case, more than 5½% per annum.	Compulsory for all State and private banks.	Annually ¼ of 1% until fund equaled 1½% of base. Resumed whenever fund reduced to 1% of base.	In cash immediately from fund. If fund deficient, Commissioner to issue certificates of indebtedness at 5% and not to exceed 7% if sold to secure cash for depositors.

North Dakota Act of 1917 as amended or modified 1923	All deposits not otherwise secured and on which interest was within limits specified by law.	Compulsory for every corporation in business of receiving deposits or buying and selling exchange except national banks.	Annually $\frac{1}{20}$ of 1% until fund equaled 2% of base. If fund reduced to 1½% of base, assessments resumed. Special assessments at same rate at option of Bank Commissioners, not to exceed four per year.	In cash from fund after certification of net amounts due depositors. If fund deficient, in certificates of indebtedness.
Washington Act of 1917 as amended or modified 1921	Deposits subject to check or other forms of withdrawal and not otherwise secured. Payment of interest at rates higher than authorized by guaranty fund board subjected bank to loss of insurance.	Voluntary for all State banks including trust companies but excluding mutual savings banks.	Annually $\frac{1}{10}$ of 1% until fund equaled 3% of base. If fund reduced, special assessments not to exceed ½ of 1% in any one year.	In warrants on fund issued on proof of claim; if fund deficient warrants to bear 5% interest until paid.

[1] National banks were prohibited from participating in State insurance plans by ruling in July 1908 of Attorney General of the United States.
[2] In terms of percentage of average daily insured deposits for preceding calendar year, unless otherwise noted. Excludes initial payments or contributions where applicable.
[3] The banking laws of Oklahoma were codified, revised and reenacted May 25, 1908, with little change in guaranty law.
[4] Special assessments in addition to regular annual assessment authorized 1914-1916.

Source: Federal Deposit Insurance Corporation, *Annual Report*, 1952 (1953), pp. 68-69.

Mississippi law stipulated that if the insurance fund was insufficient to pay the depositors, they were to be paid *pro rata*, and the remainder paid from subsequent assessments.

In the remaining six states the deposit insurance law provided for immediate cash reimbursement by the fund, either in full or to whatever extent was practical. In most instances provision was also made for the issuance of certificates of indebtedness in the event there was insufficient money in the fund.

Role of bank supervision. A majority of the eight states granted authority to regulate banks.[12] Semiannual bank examinations were the norm. Banking officials could enforce capital requirements and issue cease-and-desist orders to bring about correction of various infractions. In four of the states, supervisory authorities could order the removal of bank officials for just cause.

Despite the powers granted to banking authorities, supervision often proved to be lax. Because of understaffing and insufficient funding, examiner workloads frequently were untenable. In other instances banking authorities were thwarted when they tried to enforce existing laws. In a few cases the authorities were the root of the problem. Oklahoma provided the worst example in that the bank commissioner's office itself became corrupt after 1919.

Assessments on participating banks. All of the insurance programs derived the bulk of their income from assessments. Both regular and special assessments were based on total deposits. The assessments levied ranged from an amount equivalent to an average annual rate of about one-eighth of one percent in Kansas to about two-thirds of one percent in Texas. Some states permitted participating banks to retain their insurance assessments in the form of deposits, subject to withdrawal by order of the insurer. Other states provided for the physical collection of assessments by the insurer or the state treasurer.

Adequacy and termination of insurance funds. The state insurance funds were unable to cope with the economic events of the 1920s. The depression of 1921, and the severe agricultural problems that persisted throughout much of the decade, resulted in numerous bank failures. The resultant claims on the various insurance funds generally exceeded their size. While the Texas fund was able to meet all claims, the insured deposits in the other states that were never paid from any source ranged as high as 70 percent.

---

[12]An in-depth discussion of the role of bank supervision appears in Clark Warburton's study, *Deposit Insurance in Eight States During the Period 1908-1930* (Washington, D.C.: Federal Deposit Insurance Corporation, 1959).

The first fund to cease operations was Washington's in 1921. By early 1930, all of the funds, including the Texas fund, which became insolvent after most of the participating banks withdrew, had ceased operations.

Congressional Proposals for Deposit Guaranty or Insurance, 1886-1933

A total of 150 proposals for deposit insurance or guaranty were made in Congress between 1886 and the establishment of the Federal Deposit Insurance Corporation in 1933. Financial crises prompted the introduction of many of these proposals. In the 60th Congress, following the panic of 1907, more than thirty proposals for deposit guaranty legislation were introduced. Similarly, in response to the developing banking crisis, more than twenty bills were introduced in the 72nd Congress, which opened in 1931.

Another group of bills, similar in principle to deposit insurance, proposed to authorize national banks to issue circulating notes on the basis of various types of assets or as general obligations of the banks, backed by a guaranty or insurance fund to which all national banks would contribute. These proposals were numerous during the thirty years preceding establishment of the Federal Reserve System in 1913.

Three general methods of providing depositor protection were proposed in the bills. Of the 150 bills, 118 provided for the establishment of an insurance fund out of which depositors' losses would be paid, 22 provided for United States government guaranty of deposits, and 10 required banks to purchase surety bonds guaranteeing deposits in full.

Most of the deposit insurance bills introduced prior to establishment of the Federal Reserve System authorized participation of national banks only. After 1913, about one-half of the deposit insurance bills provided for participation of all members of the Federal Reserve System (national and state member banks). Only a few provided for coverage of deposits in nonmember banks, and then participation was usually optional.

Nearly two-thirds of the bills introduced prior to establishment of the Federal Reserve System provided for administration of the insurance system by the Comptroller of the Currency. After 1913, some of the proposals provided for administration by the Federal Reserve Board or by the Federal Reserve Banks under supervision of the Board. Other proposals called for the establishment of a special administrative board to oversee the insurance system.

Eighty percent of the bills provided for insurance or guaranty of all, or nearly all, deposits. The bills that provided for only partial coverage of deposits contained a variety of limitations. Generally, all liabilities not otherwise secured were to be protected by the insurance or guaranty system.

In nearly one-half of the bills the entire cost of deposit insurance, and in about one-fourth of the bills the major part of the cost, was to be met by assessments based upon total deposits or average total deposits. The rates of assessment ranged from one-fiftieth of one percent to one-half of one percent per year, while in a number of cases assessments were to be adjusted to meet the total cost. The most common rate was one-tenth of one percent. Many of the bills provided for special initial assessments, or for assessments as needed, in addition to those collected periodically.

In a number of bills, assessments upon the banks were to be supplemented by appropriations from the United States government, or, particularly in the bills introduced in the later years, by levies on the earnings or surplus of the Federal Reserve Banks. In several cases the cost was to be met solely by the United States government. In cases where the insurance was in the form of surety bonds, the cost of the bonds was to be borne by the banks.

Many of the bills called for a limit on the accumulation of funds by the insurance or guaranty system. In a few bills, assessment rates were to be adjusted by the administrative authority and were required to be sufficient to meet all losses to depositors or to maintain the fund at a given size. In some proposals, the fund was authorized to borrow if necessary, and in others to issue certificates to unpaid depositors if the fund were depleted.

Summary

The disruption caused by bank failures was a recurrent problem during the 19th century and the first third of the 20th century. Numerous plans were proposed or adopted to address this problem. Many embodied the insurance principle.

Insurance of bank obligations by the states occurred during two distinct periods. The first began in 1829 with the adoption of an insurance plan by New York. During the next three decades five other states followed New York's lead. Except for Michigan's insurance plan, which failed after a short period of operation, these plans accomplished their purposes. Nevertheless, the last of these insurance programs went out of existence in 1866 when the great majority of state-chartered banks became national banks.

Insurance of bank obligations was not attempted again by the states until the early 1900s. Eight states established deposit guaranty funds between 1907 and 1917. In contrast to the earlier state insurance systems, those adopted between 1907 and 1917 were generally unsuccessful. Most of the eight insurance plans were particularly hard hit by the agricultural depression that followed World War I. The numerous bank failures spawned by that depression placed severe financial stress on the insurance funds. By the mid-1920s, all of the state insurance programs were in difficulty and by early 1930 none remained in operation.

The federal government, in turn, sought to secure the safety of the circulating medium through direct guarantee by the Treasury of national bank notes, beginning in the 1860s. However, the subsequent rapid growth of bank deposits relative to bank notes once again aroused concern regarding the safety of the circulating medium in the event of a bank failure. Consequently, 150 proposals for deposit insurance or guaranty were introduced into Congress between 1886 and 1933.

The basic principles of the federal deposit insurance system were developed in these bills and in the experience of the various states that adopted insurance programs. These principles included financing the federal deposit insurance fund through assessments, the use of rigorous bank examination and supervision to limit the exposure of the fund, and other elements, such as standards for failed bank payoffs and liquidations, intended to minimize the economic disruptions caused by bank failures.

Chapter 3
Establishment
of the
FDIC

The adoption of nationwide deposit insurance in 1933 was made possible by the times, by the perseverance of the Chairman of the House Committee on Banking and Currency, and by the fact that the legislation attracted support from two groups which formerly had divergent aims and interests — those who were determined to end destruction of circulating medium due to bank failures and those who sought to preserve the existing banking structure.[1]

Banking Developments, 1930-1932

An average of more than 600 banks per year failed between 1921 and 1929, which was ten times the rate of failure during the preceding decade. The closings evoked relatively little concern, however, because they primarily involved small, rural banks, many of which were thought to be badly managed and weak. Although these failures caused the demise of the state insurance programs by early 1930, the prevailing view apparently was that the disappearance of these banks served to strengthen the banking system.

This ambivalence disappeared after a wave of bank failures during the last few months of 1930 triggered widespread attempts to convert deposits to cash. Many banks, seeking to accommodate cash demands or increase liquidity, contracted credit and, in some cases, liquidated assets. This reduced the quantity of cash available to the community which, in turn, placed additional cash demands on banks. Banks were forced to restrict credit and liquidate assets, further depressing asset prices and exacerbating liquidity problems. As more banks were unable to meet withdrawals and were closed, depositors became more sensitive to rumors. Confidence in the banking system began to erode and bank "runs" became more common.

During this period, the Federal Reserve did little to ease the liquidity problems of banks. The failure of the Federal Reserve

---

[1]Golembe, "The Deposit Insurance Legislation of 1933," p. 182.

This 1931 cartoon was awarded a Pulitzer Prize the following year.

Photo: Reprinted by permission: Tribune Company Syndicate, Inc.

to adopt an aggressive stance with respect to either open market purchases of securities or its discount window operations has been ascribed to several factors.[2] Most notably, it was generally believed that bank failures were an outgrowth of bad management and, therefore, were not subject to corrective action by the Federal Reserve. Concern within the System also was muted because most failed banks in 1930 were nonmembers for which Federal Reserve officials felt no responsibility.

In all, 1,350 banks suspended operations during 1930 (Table 3-1).[3] Bank failures during the previous decade had been confined primarily to agricultural areas; this no longer was the case in 1930. In fact, the Bank of United States, one of the nation's largest banks based in New York City, failed that year. The large jump in bank failures in 1930 was accompanied by an even greater increase in depositor losses (Table 3-1).

As liquidity pressures subsequently eased during the early months of 1931, the number of bank failures declined sharply but the decrease proved to be short-lived. Bank failures again rose between March and June as the public resumed converting deposits into currency and banks sought to meet withdrawal demands. During the second-half of the year, another, more serious, liquidity scramble occurred.

Once again, the Federal Reserve failed to inject sufficient liquidity into the banking system. In 1931, policymakers were primarily preoccupied with international monetary matters. The abandonment by Great Britain of the gold standard in September 1931 aroused general fears that other countries might follow. These fears caused many foreigners with U.S. bank accounts to convert deposits to gold in the New York money market. To stem the ensuing gold outflow, the Reserve Bank of New York

---

[2]A discussion of the Federal Reserve System's attitude appears in Milton Friedman and Anna J. Schwartz, *A Monetary History of the United States, 1867-1960* (Princeton, New Jersey: National Bureau of Economic Research, 1963), pp. 357-359. Much of the discussion relating to the events preceding the nationwide bank holiday is based on this source.

[3]The terms "bank suspensions" and "bank failures" are often used interchangeably. For the most part, this practice is followed throughout the chapter. Technically, however, "suspensions" include all banks that are closed because of financial difficulties, whereas "failures" are limited to those suspended banks that were placed in the hands of receivers and liquidated. Some of the suspended banks were reorganized or restored to solvency and resumed operations. In either instance, the assumption is that the suspended bank actually failed, though rehabilitation later occurred.

Table 3-1.   Commercial Bank Suspensions, 1921-1933 ($ Thousands)

Year	Number of Suspensions (1)	Deposits (2)	Losses Borne by Depositors (3)	Losses to Depositors As a Percent of Deposits in All Commerical Banks (4)
1921	506	$172,806	$59,967	0.21%
1922	366	91,182	38,223	0.13
1923	646	149,601	62,142	0.19
1924	775	210,150	79,381	0.23
1925	617	166,937	60,799	0.16
1926	975	260,153	83,066	0.21
1927	669	199,332	60,681	0.15
1928	498	142,386	43,813	0.10
1929	659	230,643	76,659	0.18
1930	1,350	837,096	237,359	0.57
1931	2,293	1,690,232	390,476	1.01
1932	1,453	706,187	168,302	0.57
1933	4,000	3,596,708	540,396	2.15

Source: Columns (1), (2), (3), FDIC; Column (4), Friedman and Schwartz.

sharply increased its rediscount rate. While this action achieved the desired effect, no steps were taken to augment already depleted bank reserves through extensive open market purchases of securities. By ignoring domestic financial considerations, the Federal Reserve added to the banking industry's woes.

The effects of these liquidity crises were reflected in the failure statistics. About 2,300 banks suspended operations in 1931 (Table 3-1). The number of failures thus exceeded the average number for the 1921-1929 period by almost threefold. Losses borne by depositors in 1931 exceeded losses for the entire 1921-1929 period.

In an attempt to ease bank liquidity problems, a National Credit Corporation, organized by bankers in the private sector, was created in October 1931 to extend loans to weakened banks. However, the corporation failed within a matter of weeks. Business leaders appealed to the federal government for assistance. The Hoover Administration responded by recommending two measures. The first resulted in the creation, in January 1932, of a new major federal lending agency, the Reconstruction Finance Corporation (RFC). One of its primary functions was to make advances to banks. By the end of 1932, the RFC had authorized almost $900 million in loans to assist over 4,000 banks striving to remain open. The RFC might have assisted more banks had Congress not ordered it to disclose publicly the names of borrowers, beginning in August 1932. Appearance of a bank's name on the list was interpreted as a sign of weakness, and frequently led to runs on the bank. Consequently, many banks refrained from borrowing from the RFC.

The second measure supported by the Hoover Administration, the Glass-Steagall Act of February 27, 1932, broadened the circumstances under which member banks could borrow from the Federal Reserve System. It enabled a member bank to borrow from a Federal Reserve Bank upon paper other than that ordinarily eligible for rediscount or as collateral for loans. While the amounts subsequently borrowed were not large in the aggregate, the measure did aid individual banks.

The generally improved banking situation during the ensuing months was marked by a significant drop in both the number of bank failures and depositor losses. Other signs suggested that the industry's troubles were far from over. Waves of bank failures still occurred during the year. Another disquieting sign was the emergence of bank moratoria. Initially, they were declared by individual local communities. Later that year, Nevada proclaimed the first statewide moratorium when runs on individual banks threatened to involve banks throughout the state. Similar moratoria were to play a role in the events that culminated in the nationwide bank holiday of 1933.

The Banking Crisis of 1933

During the winter of 1932-1933, banking conditions deteriorated rapidly. In retrospect, it is not possible to point to any single factor that precipitated the calamitous events of this period. The general uncertainty with respect to monetary and banking conditions undoubtedly played the major role, although there were specific events that tended to increase liquidity pressures within the system. Banks, especially in states that had declared bank moratoria, accelerated withdrawals from correspondents in an attempt to strengthen their position. Currency holdings increased significantly, partially in anticipation of additional bank moratoria.

Additional liquidity pressures were brought about by concern relating to the future of the dollar. With the election of Franklin D. Roosevelt in November 1932, rumors circulated that the new administration would devalue, which led to an increase in speculative holdings of foreign currencies, gold and gold certificates. Unlike the period of international monetary instability in

1931, a significant amount of the conversions from Federal Reserve Notes and deposits to gold came from domestic sources. These demands placed considerable strain on New York City banks and, ultimately, on the Federal Reserve Bank of New York.

It was the suddenness of the withdrawal demands in selected parts of the country that started a panic of massive proportions. State after state declared bank holidays. The banking panic reached a peak during the first three days of March 1933. Visitors arriving in Washington to attend the presidential inauguration found notices in their hotel rooms that checks drawn on out-of-town banks would not be honored. By March 4, Inauguration Day, every state in the Union had declared a bank holiday.

As one of his first official acts, President Roosevelt proclaimed a nationwide bank holiday to commence on March 6 and last four days. Administration officials quickly began to draft legislation designed to legalize the holiday and resolve the banking crisis. Early in their deliberations they realized that the success of any proposed plan of action primarily would hinge on favorable public reaction. As noted by Raymond Moley, a key presidential adviser who attended many of the planning sessions:

> We knew how much of banking depended upon make-believe or, stated more conservatively, the vital part that public confidence had in assuring solvency.[4]

To secure public support, officials formulated a plan that relied on orthodox banking procedures.

Few members of Congress knew what was contained in the Administration's bill when they convened in extraordinary session at noon on March 9. In fact, Henry B. Steagall, Chairman of the Committee on Banking and Currency, purportedly had the only copy of the bill in the House. Waving the copy over his head, Steagall had entered the House chamber, shouting, "Here's the bill. Let's pass it."[5] After only 40 minutes of debate, during which time no amendments were permitted, the House passed the bill, known as the Emergency Banking Act. Several hours later, the Senate also approved the emergency legislation intact.

---

[4]Raymond Moley, *The First New Deal* (New York: Harcourt, Brace & World, Inc., 1966), p. 171.

[5]Ibid., p. 177.

The Emergency Banking Act legalized the national bank holiday and set standards for the reopening of banks after the holiday. The Act expanded the RFC's powers as a means of dealing with the crisis then threatening the banking system. It authorized the RFC to invest in the preferred stock and capital notes of banks and to make secured loans to individual banks.

To insure an adequate supply of currency, the Act provided for the issuance of Federal Reserve Notes, which were to be backed by U.S. government securities. The Federal Reserve Banks were empowered to advance the new currency to member banks without requiring much collateral. After the Act was signed into law, the Bureau of Engraving and Printing promptly went into 24-hour production to manufacture the currency.

The President subsequently issued a proclamation extending the holiday in order to allow time for officials to reopen the banks. In his first "fireside chat," delivered on March 12, President Roosevelt reviewed the events of the past several days and outlined the reopening schedule. Following proper certification, member banks in the twelve Federal Reserve Bank cities were to reopen on March 13. Member banks in some 250 other cities with recognized clearinghouses were to reopen on March 14. Thereafter, licensed member banks in all other localities were to reopen. The President indicated that the Secretary of the Treasury already had contacted the various state banking departments and requested them to follow the same schedule in reopening state nonmember banks. Before concluding his radio address, the President cautioned that he could not promise that every bank in the nation would be reopened. About 4,000 banks never reopened either because of the events of the previous two months or the bank holiday itself.

The task of implementing the Emergency Banking Act primarily was the responsibility of the Secretary of the Treasury. Under the Act, licenses for all member banks, both national and state, were to be issued by the Secretary. (State nonmember banks were to be licensed by the state banking departments.) The Treasury, however, demanded that each of the Federal Reserve Banks approve of the reopening of banks in their respective districts. The Federal Reserve Board balked at this demand, preferring instead that the Treasury Department shoulder the entire burden of reopening member banks. The controversy was resolved in the Treasury Department's favor. It was agreed that licenses would be issued by the Secretary of the Treasury upon the recommendation of the district Federal Reserve Bank, the chief national bank examiner and the Comptroller of the Currency. Several hundred banks soon reopened for business on the certification of the Treasury. As the reopenings proceeded, public confidence increased significantly and widespread hoarding ceased.

Federal Deposit Insurance Legislation

After some semblance of order had returned to the financial system, efforts were renewed in Congress to enact deposit insurance legislation. Although a deposit insurance bill had been passed by the House in 1932, the Senate had adjourned without acting on the proposal. Insurance proponents hoped that legislative efforts would prove successful this time, since the banking crisis was still fresh in the public's mind. In their view, recent events had shown that a system of federal deposit insurance was necessary to achieve and maintain financial stability.

One of the chief proponents of federal deposit insurance in Congress was Representative Henry B. Steagall. He has been credited with proposing the legislation which created the Federal Deposit Insurance Corporation, leading the fight for its adoption in the House and helping to effect a compromise when chances for passage of the bill appeared doomed. Steagall's achievement was all the more remarkable in view of the formidable opposition confronting the proponents of deposit insurance. Opposition emanated from the Roosevelt Administration, segments of the banking industry and from some members of Congress.

Arguments offered against deposit insurance reflected both practical and philosophical considerations. Opponents asserted that deposit insurance would never work. They pointed to the defunct state-level deposit programs to substantiate their argument. Another widely held view was that deposit insurance would remove penalties for bad management. Critics also charged that deposit insurance would be too expensive and that it would represent an unwarranted intrusion by the federal government into the private sector.

Within the Roosevelt Administration, the Secretary of the Treasury was strongly opposed to the idea of federal deposit insurance. While historians have asserted that Secretary Woodin's views were partially responsible for President Roosevelt's opposition to deposit insurance, accounts differ regarding the nature and extent of Franklin Roosevelt's opposition. However, the Administration was not of one mind on the issue.

Support was voiced by Vice President John Nance Garner and Jesse H. Jones of the RFC, among others. Prior to Roosevelt's inauguration, Garner, then-Speaker of the House, had appealed to the President-elect to support deposit insurance. When Roosevelt declined, stating that it would never work, Garner predicted that deposit insurance legislation eventually would be passed.[6]

Banking interests, particularly those representing the larger banks, generally viewed federal deposit insurance with distaste. The President of the American Bankers Association declared that deposit insurance was "unsound, unscientific and dangerous."[7] The banking industry's views had only limited impact since banking at that time was held in low esteem. The industry's already tarnished image was not helped by disclosures of unsavory security market dealings on the part of certain New York banks which came to light when deposit insurance was being considered in Congress.

More formidable opposition to deposit insurance came from several influential Congressmen. One of the most vociferous opponents was Carter Glass of Virginia, Chairman of the Senate Banking and Currency Committee. He had been Roosevelt's initial choice to serve as Secretary of the Treasury, but declined the Cabinet offer. Although Senator Glass was intent on passing banking reform legislation, federal deposit insurance was not one of the reforms he supported or sought. In opposing federal deposit insurance, Glass pointed to the record of the defunct state insurance programs. Nevertheless, he subsequently allowed bank deposit insurance to be written into a banking bill that he had sponsored. One business journal during the period reported that Glass simply had yielded to public opinion:

> It became perfectly apparent that the voters wanted the guarantee [deposit insurance], and that no bill which did not contain such a provision would be satisfactory either to Congress or to the public. Washington does not remember any issue on which the sentiment of the country has been so undivided or so emphatically expressed as upon this.[8]

In mid-May, both Senator Glass and Representative Steagall formally introduced banking reform bills, which included provisions for deposit insurance. The two bills primarily differed

---

[6]Ibid., pp. 318-319.

[7]"Wires Banks to Urge Veto of Glass Bill," *New York Times*, June 16, 1933, p. 14.

[8]"Deposit Insurance," *Business Week*, April 12, 1933, p. 3.

41

with respect to the conditions for membership in the deposit insurance corporation that was to be created. Whereas membership in the Federal Reserve was a precondition for obtaining deposit insurance under the Senate bill, it was not a prerequisite in the House version. Both bills incorporated the demands made by the Roosevelt Administration that: (1) deposit coverage be based on a sliding scale; and (2) there be a one-year delay in the start of the insurance corporation.

Later that month, however, the Glass bill was amended to incorporate Senator Arthur Vandenberg's proposal calling for the creation of a temporary deposit insurance fund. Vandenberg opposed a delay in the start of deposit insurance because "the need is greater in the next year than for the next hundred years."[9] On the day Vandenberg introduced his proposal, Vice President Garner was presiding over the Senate, which was sitting as a court of impeachment in the trial of a district judge. Garner had heard that Vandenberg had formulated a deposit insurance plan that would accomplish the same goals as those contained in an insurance bill which Garner had pushed through the House in 1932. Desiring that deposit insurance be implemented as soon as possible, Garner therefore approached Vandenberg during the impeachment proceedings and inquired whether he had the deposit insurance amendment in his possession. After Vandenberg responded affirmatively, Garner instructed him to introduce the amendment when signaled. Several minutes later, Garner suspended the court proceedings and ordered the Senate into regular session to consider more banking legislation. With Garner sitting by his side, Vandenberg then offered his deposit insurance amendment, which was overwhelmingly adopted.

The amendment stipulated that, effective January 1, 1934, the temporary fund would provide insurance coverage up to $2,500 for each depositor and would function until a permanent corporation began operations on July 1, 1934. If demands on the temporary fund exceeded available monies, the Treasury would be obliged to make up the difference. The amendment also provided that solvent state banks could join the fund.

The inclusion of the Vandenberg amendment in the Senate bill almost resulted in the defeat of deposit insurance in Congress. When the banking reform bills that had been passed by

---

[9]"Bank Bill Debate to Open in Senate," *New York Times,* May 19, 1933, p. 4.

both houses were sent to a joint conference committee, for resolution of differences, an impasse promptly developed. The House conferees opposed the Vandenberg amendment contained in the Senate version of the bill, particularly the provision calling for the immediate establishment of a temporary insurance corporation. Another issue that split the conferees was whether Federal Reserve membership should be a precondition for obtaining deposit insurance.

A compromise finally was reached on June 12, after the Senate conferees threatened to remove all deposit insurance provisions from the bill. They feared that the impasse over deposit insurance could endanger all of the banking reform measures contained in the bill. In order to save the bill, the House conferees reluctantly accepted the Senate's version as well as an additional provision desired by the Senate conferees to liberalize the branching restrictions governing national banks. This provision reflected widespread public disillusionment with the failure-prone independent banking system. Proponents of branch banking maintained that geographic diversification of lending risks and the deposit base would result in a lower bank failure rate.

The bill agreed to by the conferees passed both houses of Congress on the following day. Some opponents of deposit insurance had not yet thrown in the towel, though. The American Bankers Association wired its member banks, urging them to telegraph President Roosevelt immediately to request his veto of the legislation. Nevertheless, President Roosevelt signed the measure, known as the Banking Act of 1933, into law on June 16, 1933. Section 8 of the Act created the Federal Deposit Insurance Corporation through an amendment to the Federal Reserve Act. The Banking Act of 1933 also created the Federal Reserve Open Market Committee and imposed restrictions on the permissible activities of member banks of the Federal Reserve System.

Deposit Insurance Provisions of the Banking Act of 1933

Section 12B of the Federal Reserve Act as amended created the Federal Deposit Insurance Corporation and defined its organization, duties and functions. It provided for two separate plans of deposit insurance: a temporary plan which was to be initiated on January 1, 1934, and a permanent plan which was to become effective on July 1, 1934.

43

Capital necessary to establish the FDIC was to be provided by the United States Treasury and the twelve Federal Reserve Banks. The Treasury was to contribute $150 million. Each of the twelve Federal Reserve Banks was required to subscribe to Class B capital stock in an amount equal to one-half of its surplus as of January 1, 1933.

Management of the FDIC was vested in a Board of Directors consisting of three members. The Comptroller of the Currency was designated a member *ex officio;* the other two members were to be appointed by the President for six-year terms with the advice and consent of the Senate. One of the two appointive directors was to serve as Chairman of the Board, and not more than two members of the Board could be members of the same political party.

The temporary plan of deposit insurance initially limited protection to $2,500 for each depositor. Banks admitted to insurance under the temporary plan were to be assessed an amount equal to one-half of one percent of insurable deposits. One-half of the assessment was payable at once; the rest was payable upon call by the FDIC.

All Federal Reserve member banks licensed by the Secretary of the Treasury under terms of an Executive Order of the President, issued March 10, 1933, were required by law to become members of the temporary fund on January 1, 1934. Other banks were authorized to join the fund upon certification of their solvency by the respective state supervisory agencies and after examination by, and with the approval of, the Federal Deposit Insurance Corporation.

The original permanent plan, while it never took effect and was superseded by a new permanent plan in the Banking Act of 1935, contained certain features of historical interest. Banks participating in insurance under the original plan were to subscribe to capital stock of the FDIC and be subject to whatever assessments might be needed to meet the losses from deposit insurance operations. The plan provided for full protection of the first $10,000 of each depositor, 75 percent coverage of the next $40,000 of deposits, and 50 percent coverage of all deposits in excess of $50,000. In order to retain their insurance, all participating banks were required to become members of the Federal Reserve System within two years. Thus, with regard to financing, degree of protection and supervisory provisions, the original plan differed significantly from both the temporary plan and the permanent plan that became effective with the Banking Act of 1935.

44

The first Board of Directors of the Federal Deposit Insurance Corporation was sworn in at the Treasury Department, Washington, D.C., on September 11, 1933. From left, E. G. Bennett, FDIC Director; Walter J. Cummings, FDIC Chairman; J. F. T. O'Connor, Comptroller of the Currency and FDIC Board Member. Administering the oath is J. F. Douglas of the Treasury Department.

Formation of the Federal Deposit Insurance Corporation

One of the first tasks facing the FDIC was the formation of an operating organization. As provided in the Banking Act of 1933, the Comptroller of the Currency, J. F. T. O'Connor, was designated as a director. He served as the FDIC's chief executive until the appointment of the other two directors.

In September, the President appointed as the other directors Walter J. Cummings, then special assistant to Secretary of the Treasury Woodin, and E. G. Bennett, a Republican banker and businessman from Utah. The directors organized on September 11, 1933, and elected Walter J. Cummings, Chairman of the Board.[10] As was his intent, Cummings' chairmanship lasted only through the initial organization of the FDIC. In January 1934, he left the FDIC to assume the chairmanship of Continental Illinois National Bank & Trust Company in Chicago.

Bank examination consumed nearly all of the FDIC's efforts in the months prior to the establishment of the temporary fund on January 1, 1934. The hastily assembled examination force had to examine almost 8,000 state-chartered nonmember banks in three months in order for the FDIC to meet its responsibilities under the Banking Act of 1933. The task of completing these admission examinations was largely accomplished as intended by the end of 1933.

The Temporary Federal Deposit Insurance Fund

Admission standards. Actual insurance of bank deposits became effective on January 1, 1934. The Temporary Federal Deposit Insurance Fund opened with 13,201 banks insured (or approved for insurance). Of these, 12,987 were commercial banks and 214 were mutual savings banks. These represented 90 percent of all commercial banks and 36 percent of all mutual savings banks.

The lower participation rate among savings banks was attributable to several factors. Many savings banks questioned whether they needed deposit insurance. Unlike commercial banks, savings banks had not been seriously affected by bank runs since they legally could restrict deposit withdrawals. In several states mutual savings banks legally could not subscribe

---

[10]The FDIC's Boards of Directors during its first half-century are listed in the Appendix.

46

to stock in the FDIC. In other instances, savings banks objected to FDIC membership on philosophical grounds. As summed up by one savings banker: "I for one want none of this FDIC. If it's New Deal, that damns it as far as I'm concerned."[11]

Pursuant to the intent of Congress, the FDIC accepted for insurance all banks that it found to be solvent. However, it was recognized that a great many banks lacked sufficient capital, which posed a huge risk for the insurance fund. Some banks were admitted upon a commitment to increase their capital, and early in 1934 RFC and local capital was secured according to those commitments. A program of reexamination and rehabilitation was carried on throughout the year by the FDIC.

Organizational changes. Following the departure of Walter J. Cummings, E. G. Bennett served briefly as acting chairman of the FDIC. In February 1934, Leo T. Crowley, a 46-year-old bachelor, became chairman. As former owner of several Wisconsin banks during the Depression, he had organized and headed the Wisconsin Banking Review Board. In December 1933, he journeyed to Washington, D.C., seeking aid for several hundred Wisconsin banks so they could qualify for deposit insurance. His role in restoring the health of depression-struck banks in his native state brought him to the attention of the Roosevelt Administration.

The appointment of Crowley proved to be especially felicitous. An imposing man, he possessed both a witty personality and exceptional administrative skills. He left an indelible imprint on the FDIC during his twelve-year term as chairman.

Legislative developments. The Banking Act of 1933 provided for termination of the Temporary Federal Deposit Insurance Fund and the inauguration of the permanent insurance plan on July 1, 1934. However, in the early part of 1934, FDIC officials recommended that the Temporary Federal Deposit Insurance Fund be extended for another year and that the law be amended in certain minor respects to facilitate administration. It was considered advisable to give the states additional time to adopt legislation to enable state banks to enjoy the full benefits of federal deposit insurance. FDIC officials also desired to gain more experience with the administration and operation of an insurance plan prior to the inauguration of the permanent plan. Moreover, the capital rehabilitation program for banks could not have been completed by July 1934 as required to permit all

---

[11]Oscar Schisgall, *Out of One Small Chest* (New York: AMACOM, 1975), p. 146.

banks insured with the Temporary Federal Deposit Insurance Fund to qualify for insurance under the permanent plan.

On June 16, 1934, Congress extended the life of the Temporary Federal Deposit Insurance Fund, and the effective date of the permanent plan was postponed one year, to July 1, 1935.[12] Insured nonmember banks were allowed to terminate their membership in the Temporary Federal Deposit Insurance Fund on July 1, 1934, provided they gave adequate notice to the FDIC. Provision was made for refunding the assessments collected from the banks that withdrew.

There had been some doubt as to the legality of some mutual savings banks qualifying as members of the permanent plan of deposit insurance. Furthermore, many mutual savings banks considered themselves preferred risks and wished to avoid assessment at the same rate as commercial banks. For these and other reasons, 169 mutual savings banks withdrew from the Temporary Federal Deposit Insurance Fund at the end of June 1934. Of these, 133 were located in New York State. Only two New York mutual savings banks, Emigrant Savings Bank and Franklin Savings Bank, kept their insurance with the FDIC. (Only 21 commercial banks withdrew from the Fund on July 1, 1934.)

Effective July 1, 1934, insurance protection was increased from $2,500 to $5,000 for each depositor at an insured institution, except in the case of certain mutual savings banks. Insurance protection remained at $2,500 for each depositor at a mutual savings bank except that any mutual savings bank could, with the consent of the FDIC, elect to be insured up to $5,000.

The FDIC, at the discretion of its Board of Directors, was authorized to set up a separate fund for mutual savings banks to be known as the Fund For Mutuals. The Temporary Federal Deposit Insurance Fund was not to be subject to the liabilities of the Fund For Mutuals, and vice versa. A separate Fund For Mutuals was established by the Board of Directors on July 14, 1934, effective July 1, 1934. Upon inception of the permanent plan in 1935, this fund and the fund for commercial banks were consolidated.

---

[12]The life of the temporary plan was subsequently extended for an additional two months. The second extension was approved June 28, 1935, while the Banking Act of 1935 was under consideration, and was designed merely to continue the temporary plan until that Act could be approved.

Under the previously existing law, insured nonmember banks were required to apply to become members of the Federal Reserve System on or before July 1, 1936, in order to continue their insurance. With the one-year delay in the establishment of the permanent fund, this requirement was changed by pushing the date back to July 1, 1937.

Banks in the territories of Hawaii, Puerto Rico, Alaska and the Virgin Islands were made eligible for insurance. In addition, the language authorizing the FDIC to act as receiver in the case of failed insured banks was clarified. By a new provision of the law, each insured bank was required to display signs to the effect that its deposits were insured by the Federal Deposit Insurance Corporation. This practice continues today.

Deposit Insurance and Banking Developments in 1934

Total deposits in insured and uninsured licensed commercial banks increased during 1934 by about $7.2 billion dollars, or 22 percent. This growth in deposits had rarely been equaled in the past and restored to the banking system approximately half of the decline in deposits that had occurred during the preceding three years.

The growth in bank deposits was accompanied by changes in the character and quality of the assets held by insured banks. Cash, amounts due from other banks and holdings of direct obligations of the United States government increased considerably. The average quality of the assets of insured commercial banks improved as large amounts of worthless and doubtful assets were written off. Increased earnings and new capital, which was obtained from the RFC and local interests, maintained banks' capital positions. At the close of 1934, insured banks held 98 percent of the assets of all licensed commercial banks.

The liquidity buildup undertaken by banks during 1934 caused FDIC officials some concern. They feared that excessive holdings by banks of cash and government securities could stifle economic recovery. Speeches given by the FDIC's directors during that period frequently contained exhortations urging bankers to expand their loan portfolios.

Only nine insured banks and 52 uninsured licensed banks suspended operations during 1934. All but one of the insured banks and most of the uninsured licensed banks that failed during 1934 were small institutions. More than 900 banks which were not licensed after the holiday were placed in receivership or liquidation. More than half of these banks had a part of their assets and liabilities taken over by successor banks.

In its 1934 *Annual Report,* the FDIC rather modestly attributed the small number of failures of licensed banks to factors other than deposit insurance. It noted that many banks were able to survive because they had received necessary financial assistance from the RFC and other governmental agencies. Secondly, events during 1933 had weeded out many weak banks. Third, improved economic conditions also had played a role in keeping down the failure rate. The FDIC warned that the low rate of failures could not be expected to continue.

During 1934, the fierce opposition of the banking industry faded in the face of the success of deposit insurance. The industry's changed attitude was reflected in the public endorsement of the temporary insurance plan by the Executive Council of the American Bankers Association in April of that year. Public sentiment continued to support deposit insurance.

Proposals to Amend the Permanent Insurance Law

Despite the widespread acceptance accorded to deposit insurance, interested parties increasingly voiced unhappiness over various features of the insurance plan as 1934 wore on. The banking industry wanted some legal limits placed on the FDIC's assessment powers. State bankers wanted to eliminate the requirement that federally insured banks had to join the Federal Reserve System. After gaining experience with the administration of federal deposit insurance, FDIC officials also desired legislative changes.

Congressional hearings on banking reform, including deposit insurance, began in February 1935. Title I of the bill under consideration dealt with deposit insurance. The discussions of Title I centered around two issues: the appropriate deposit insurance assessment rate and Federal Reserve membership requirements for federally insured banks.

In early August, the two houses of Congress resolved their differences on changes in the assessment rate. The House conferees acquiesced to the Senate on a one-twelfth of one percent annual assessment rate on total (adjusted) deposits. Adoption of this rate, which had been recommended by the FDIC, was based upon a combination of factors. The FDIC had calculated that during the period 1865-1934, an annual average assessment rate of about one-third of one percent of total deposits would have been required to cover the actual losses on deposit balances in failed banks. However, if certain "crisis" years in which losses were unusually high were eliminated, the necessary rate would have been lowered to about one-twelfth of one percent. Adoption of the lower rate was justified on the grounds that many banking reforms and improvements had occurred to strengthen the banking system and prevent bank failures.

A compromise also was reached on the Federal Reserve membership issue. In the final conference report, which was accepted by both Houses on August 19, only insured banks with more than $1 million in deposits would be required to join the Federal Reserve System, beginning in 1941. (The membership requirement was rescinded altogether in 1939.)

The omnibus bill passed by Congress, known as the Banking Act of 1935, became effective on August 23, 1935. The Act consisted of three distinct parts: Title I related to the Federal Deposit Insurance Corporation; Title II related to the Federal Reserve System; and Title III consisted of technical amendments to existing banking laws.

Inauguration of Permanent Plan of Insurance of Bank Deposits

The Banking Act of 1935 terminated the temporary federal deposit insurance plan and inaugurated the permanent plan. It revised the entire deposit insurance law and made substantial changes in the character of the permanent plan for deposit insurance originally enacted on June 16, 1933. However, the new plan continued to limit insurance coverage to a maximum of $5,000 for each depositor at an insured institution.

The Banking Act of 1935 provided for the automatic admission to insurance under the permanent plan of all banks insured at the close of the temporary funds, except banks which signified, within 30 days, their intention to withdraw from insurance and those banks that had failed to file the required certified statement of deposits and to pay the required assessments.

Thirty-four banks insured under the temporary plan withdrew within 30 days after the close of the temporary funds. One other bank had its insurance status terminated by reason of failure to file the certified statement. Automatically admitted to insurance under the permanent plan were 14,219 banks. Of these, 14,163 were commercial banks insured in the Temporary Federal Deposit Insurance Fund and 56 were mutual savings banks insured in the Fund For Mutuals.

The 1935 Act set more rigorous standards for admission to insurance. In acting on insurance applications from new banks, the FDIC was required to consider the adequacy of the bank's capital, its future earnings prospects, the quality of its management and its usefulness in serving the convenience and needs of the community.

The annual assessment rate was set at one-twelfth of one percent of total (adjusted) deposits. The Act eliminated the requirement of stock subscriptions by insured banks.

The revised law, moreover, provided that any balances to which an insured bank was entitled, upon termination of the temporary federal deposit insurance funds, were to be credited toward the assessment to be levied under the permanent insurance plan. These balances consisted of the unused portion of assessments collected under the temporary plan. Since investment income of the temporary funds was sufficient to pay all of the operating expenses of the FDIC and cover deposit insurance losses and expenses, insured banks received a credit for the full amount of the assessments they had paid.

Insured nonmember banks were required to obtain the FDIC's approval before opening new branches or reducing their capital. The Act required all insured banks to obtain approval before merging or consolidating with noninsured institutions. The FDIC was empowered to require any insured bank to provide protection and indemnity against burglary, defalcation and other similar insurable losses. If an insured bank was found by the FDIC to have continued unsafe or unsound practices, the practices were to be reported to the appropriate supervisory authorities. A bank's insurance status could be terminated if the practices were not corrected. (A more complete discussion of the FDIC's supervisory responsibilities is found in Chapter 6.)

In order to strengthen the banking system, the FDIC was given the right to make a loan to, or purchase assets from, an open or closed insured bank to facilitate its merger or consolidation with another insured bank, if the merger would reduce the risk or avert a threatened loss to the FDIC. This power, which was first granted on a temporary basis, was later made permanent.

The FDIC was authorized to issue notes or other obligations in an amount not to exceed $975 million, and the RFC and the

Secretary of the Treasury were directed to purchase up to $500 million of these notes if the funds were needed for the payment of depositors. The FDIC has never borrowed under this provision of the Act.

The Banking Act of 1935 required the FDIC to prohibit the payment of interest on demand deposits in insured nonmember banks and to limit the rates of interest paid on savings and time deposits. The FDIC was also required to prohibit insured nonmember banks from paying any time deposit before its maturity except as prescribed by the FDIC.

In granting these and other regulatory powers to the FDIC, Congress sought to prevent unsound competition among banks. The prevailing philosophy was that unfettered competition in the past had resulted in excesses and abuses in banking as well as other industries. The restrictive powers contained in the Banking Act of 1935 were thus consistent with the tenor of other New Deal legislative programs.

Chapter 4
Insurance Coverage and Financial Operations of the FDIC

The past 50 years have witnessed many changes in the operations of the FDIC. Some have been the result of legislation, while others have been due to the experience gained in providing deposit insurance. In retrospect, the changes have been relatively minor considering the economic climate and the level of experience with deposit insurance prevailing in 1933. This chapter focuses on the changes in the financial and internal operations of the FDIC since 1933.

Financial Operations

Many informed observers in 1933 felt that a system of federal deposit insurance, especially if substantive coverage were provided to virtually all banks, could not remain viable without direct support from the Treasury. The banking crisis of the early 1930s had left the banking system in a weakened condition. There was concern that another banking crisis could result in an accelerating rate of bank failures, and that already low bank earnings would not be sufficient to finance a deposit insurance system. At the same time, the use of tax revenues to finance a deposit insurance scheme was viewed as unacceptable, and in fact formed one of the primary bases for the Roosevelt Administration's opposition to federal deposit insurance.

The concern regarding federal involvement in financing deposit insurance led to an initial organization that closely paralleled a typical casualty insurance company. Because of the weakened condition of the banking system, however, it was recognized that at least some of the initial capitalization would have to be supplied from government sources. It was anticipated, although with some reservations on the part of many, that expenses, losses and future additions to reserves (net worth) would be covered by insurance premiums levied on insured banks and by income from investments.

As discussed in Chapter 3, the 1933 Act provided for two deposit insurance plans: a temporary plan and a permanent plan. Funding to support the temporary plan was provided by an assessment of one-half of one percent of total *insured* deposits, half of which was payable upon admittance to the program and the remainder subject to call by the FDIC. If this proved to be inadequate to cover expenses and losses, the FDIC had the authority to levy one additional assessment not to exceed the amounts already paid by insured banks. The Act also provided for one reassessment based on changes in insured deposits during the existence of the interim plan.

The financing of the permanent plan was somewhat more complex and potentially very burdensome to the banking system. Basically, the system would have involved an initial capital contribution (capital stock purchase) upon joining the program and an assessment (insurance premium) effectively to pass all insurance losses directly to insured institutions.[1] The basis for both the initial contribution and subsequent assessments was to have been shifted from insured deposits to total deposit liabilities.

During the 20 months that the Temporary Federal Deposit Insurance Fund was in operation, the banking situation improved significantly. Attention thus shifted to the specific insurance provisions of the 1933 Act. Most of those who had originally opposed deposit insurance legislation apparently had been convinced that the existence of the FDIC was a major contributing factor to the drastic reduction in bank failures. However, various provisions of the original permanent plan were viewed as not being appropriate in the new environment.

The banking industry did not like the potential for virtually unlimited assessments and generally felt that the assessment rate should be set at a relatively low level. Large banks took exception to shifting the assessment base from insured to total deposits, contending that they would be unduly penalized because of the relatively large portion of uninsured deposits held in larger institutions. State chartered, nonmember banks objected to mandatory membership in the Federal Reserve System as a precondition for retaining deposit insurance coverage.

---

[1]All capital stock issued by the FDIC was non-voting; shares issued to the Federal Reserve Banks (Class B) paid no dividends, while those that were to be issued to member banks (Class A) and issued to the U.S. Treasury carried a 6 percent, cumulative dividend rate.

For its part, the FDIC was faced with a dilemma. Although the bank failure rate had dropped precipitously and the capital rehabilitation program of the RFC and FDIC had been moderately successful, the banking system was not strong and the prospects for bank earnings were not bright. Additionally, the fears and uncertainties regarding the bank failure rate had not been dispelled by 1934 and indeed would not recede for more than two decades. The FDIC thus was faced with the problems of protecting the earnings of insured banks until capital and reserve positions could be rebuilt while, at the same time, conserving what was by historical standards a modest deposit insurance fund.

During 1934, FDIC staff began drafting what was to become Title I of the Banking Act of 1935. In hearings beginning in February 1935 before the House Committee on Banking and Currency, FDIC Chairman Leo Crowley articulated his plan for the future of federal deposit insurance. In addition to an assessment rate lower than historical experience would suggest, his plan consisted of a combination of stricter entrance standards for new banks and expanded authority over the actions of existing banks, expanded powers regarding the handling of failing banks, a reduction in insurance exposure (*i.e.*, retention of the $5,000 insurance coverage rather than the higher limit envisaged in the original permanent plan) and other provisions that would tend to conserve the deposit insurance fund.[2] From a practical point of view, the program advocated by Mr. Crowley consisted of attempting to strengthen the banking system, while using every legal means available to conserve FDIC financial resources. This philosophy dominated FDIC behavior until the mid-1960s.

The deposit insurance provisions of the Banking Act of 1935, with few exceptions, were identical to the draft legislation prepared by the FDIC. From a financial point of view, one of the most significant revisions to the original permanent plan related to the calculation of assessments levied on insured banks. The 1935 Act provided that assessments were to be based on a flat annual rate of one-twelfth of one percent of *total* deposits; the net effect of this change was to shift the relative burden of the deposit insurance system to the larger banks while protecting the

---

[2]For a more detailed discussion of the provisions of the Banking Act of 1935, see Chapter 3.

level of assessment income to the FDIC. Additionally, the requirement for initial and subsequent capital subscriptions by insured banks was deleted, and the payment of dividends on capital stock held by the U.S. Treasury was eliminated. To provide for emergency situations, the FDIC was given authority to borrow up to $975 million from the Treasury.[3]

By year-end 1946, the deposit insurance fund (net worth) had increased to over $1 billion. Because of the highly liquid condition of the banking industry, the legislation passed in the 1930s to reduce risks in many sectors of the economy and the recent low bank failure rate, many observers felt that a $1 billion fund was sufficient to cover almost any economic contingency. In fact, three years later, in connection with the Congressional hearings relating to the Federal Deposit Insurance Act of 1950, Jesse Jones, former chairman of the RFC, advocated an effective assessment rate that would maintain the deposit insurance fund at the $1 billion level. Apparently, Congress felt that the fund was adequate at that time and legislatively mandated repayment of the original capital subscriptions. The $289 million initially subscribed by the Treasury and the Federal Reserve Banks was fully repaid by the end of 1948.

Bankers also had voiced concern that the assessment rate was too high. By 1950, the deposit insurance fund had reached a level of over $1.2 billion, despite the repayment of capital completed two years earlier. Assessment income had been growing at a high rate, reflecting the rapid growth in bank deposits during the World War II and post-war years. Moreover, because of low interest rates during this same period, bank earnings lagged increases in prices and deposit insurance expenses.

The FDIC was reluctant to support a permanent reduction in the basic assessment rate. There still was concern that accumulated earnings would be insufficient to handle the increased rate of bank failures that many thought would occur during the 1950s. This fear was reinforced by the decrease in capitalization

---

[3]The 1933 Act explicitly authorized the FDIC to issue " . . . notes, debentures, bonds, or other similar obligations . . ." necessary to conduct insurance operations. The 1935 Act *directed* the Secretary of the Treasury to purchase, under certain conditions, up to $500 million of these obligations, and *authorized* the Secretary to purchase up to an additional $475 million if deemed necessary. In 1947, the specific authority of the FDIC to issue obligations was deleted, and the FDIC was given authority to borrow up to $3 billion directly from the Treasury. The FDIC has never exercised this authority.

On September 9, 1947, FDIC Chairman Maple Harl (right) presented to Under Secretary of the Treasury A.L.M Wiggins a check for $146 million, repaying more than half of the government's initial funding of the FDIC. The balance was repaid in 1948.

Photo: Harris & Ewing

59

of the banking industry due to low earnings and rapid asset expansion since 1940.

As a compromise, deposit insurance charges were effectively reduced by the Federal Deposit Insurance Act of 1950. Rather than lowering the basic assessment rate, however, the reduction was accomplished through a rebate system. After deducting operating expenses and insurance losses from gross assessment income, 40 percent was to be retained by the FDIC, with the remainder to be rebated to insured banks. This procedure meant that losses were to be shared by insured banks and the FDIC on a 60 percent - 40 percent basis. This provision has tended to stabilize FDIC earnings during periods of fluctuating loss experience.

The 1950 Act also required the FDIC to reimburse the Treasury for interest foregone on the initial capital contributions. This requirement was the result of an exchange between FDIC Chairman Maple T. Harl and Senator Paul Douglas of Illinois during hearings on the 1950 Act. The exchange went as follows:

> Senator Douglas: . . . Mr. Harl, on page 2 [of your prepared statement] you speak of making final payment to the Treasury on August 30, 1948, when you paid the Treasury out in full for the loans [capital] which were advanced. Do I understand that to be your statement?
>
> Mr. Harl: We paid them for the money advanced.
>
> Senator Douglas: Would that include the interest upon the Goverment loan which was made?
>
> Mr. Harl: It did not. The law provided that there should be no dividend upon the capital stock.
>
> Senator Douglas: In practice, the Government has made an advance to the FDIC which has not been repaid; namely, the interest on the bonds which the Government issued, but for which it was not reimbursed.
>
> . . .
>
> Mr. Harl: . . . This Corporation stands ready to reimburse the Government, or anyone else, provided it is legally authorized to do so.
>
> Senator Douglas: You are ready to pay the interest, is that right?
>
> Mr. Harl: Yes. If we have an obligation we are ready to pay it.
>
> . . .
>
> Senator Douglas: That is a possible source of revenue that I had not thought of. This brief conversation, which I at first thought was going to be unprofitable, might yield the Government as much as $40,000,000. I first thought it was love's labor lost. It may turn out that there was gold in "them there hills."[4]

---

[4] U.S., Congress, Senate, Committee on Banking and Currency, *Hearings before a subcommittee of the Senate Committee on Banking and Currency on Bills to Amend the Federal Deposit Insurance Act*, 81st Cong., 2d sess., January 11, 23 and 30, 1950, pp. 27-29.

During 1950 and 1951, the FDIC paid about $81 million to the Treasury for the interest foregone on the initial contribution of both the Treasury and the Federal Reserve Banks.[5]

The 1950 Act also removed the law governing FDIC operations from the Federal Reserve Act, and created a separate body of law known as the Federal Deposit Insurance Act. Although of only symbolic significance, this change over the years has reinforced the FDIC's separate identity.

To compensate certain banks for the effect of a technical change in the computation of the assessment base, net assessments were further reduced in 1960, when the rebate percentage was increased to 66⅔ percent. In 1980, the basic percentage was lowered to 60 percent, with mandatory adjustments to be made if the ratio of the deposit insurance fund to estimated "insured" deposits were to exceed 1.40 percent or were less than 1.10 percent. The FDIC sought this latter provision to help rebuild the fund if abnormally high losses were experienced, and to inhibit excessive growth of the fund in periods of low losses.

Income and Expenses of the FDIC

The major sources of income to the FDIC have been assessments collected from insured banks and interest on its portfolio of U.S. Treasury securities. In recent years, interest on capital notes advanced to facilitate mergers and deposit assumption transactions and to assist open insured banks has become an increasing, although not major, source of income.

Expenses incurred by the FDIC are normally grouped into two categories. Administrative expenses include expenditures not directly attributable to bank closings and the subsequent liquidation of assets. The other major expense category, insurance expenses and losses, includes expenses associated with bank closings, liquidation activities and the FDIC's share of losses on acquired assets.

Table 4-1 presents the major income and expense items for each year since 1933. For over half of this period, assessments accounted for the largest share of income to the FDIC. However, continued favorable loss experience allowed the securities portfolio to grow so that, in 1961, investment income exceeded assessments. This relationship has continued since that time and, absent abnormally large cash demands or drastic reductions

---

[5]The rate was set by statute at two percent per annum.

Table 4-1. FDIC Income and Expenses, 1934-1982 ($ Millions)

	Deposit Insurance Assessments[1]	Investment Income	Other Income	Administrative Expenses	Insurance Losses & Expenses	Net Income
1982	1,012.7	1,370.0	142.0	129.9	869.9	1,524.8
1981	921.9	1,115.5	37.3	127.2	720.9	1,226.6
1980	430.8	863.1	16.5	118.2	(34.6)	1,226.8
1979	356.4	704.3	29.7	106.8	(13.1)	996.7
1978	367.0	565.8	19.3	103.3	45.6	803.2
1977	319.4	503.2	15.3	89.3	24.3	724.2
1976	296.5	449.7	18.7	180.4[3]	31.9	552.6
1975	278.9	394.3	16.1	67.7	29.8	591.8
1974	302.0	357.8	8.6	59.2	100.0	508.9
1973	246.0	311.1	4.0	54.4	53.8	452.8
1972	188.5	277.0	1.5	49.6	10.1	407.3
1971	175.8	239.1	.400	46.9	13.4	355.0
1970	159.3	222.7	.647	42.2	3.8	336.7
1969	144.0	191.7	.031	33.5	1.0	301.3
1968	132.4	162.6	(.015)	29.0	0.1	265.9
1967	120.7	142.3	.008	24.4	2.9	235.7
1966	111.7	129.3	.002	19.8	0.1	221.1
1965	102.2	112.3	.202	17.7	5.2	191.7
1964	93.0	104.1	.010	15.5	2.9	178.7
1963	84.2	97.5	.064	14.4	0.7	166.8
1962	76.5	84.6	.031	13.7	0.1	147.3
1961	73.4	73.8	.021	13.2	1.6	132.5
1960	79.6	64.9	.132	12.4	0.1	132.1
1959	78.6	57.8	.020	11.9	0.2	124.4
1958	73.8	53.1	.015	11.6	. . .	115.2
1957	69.1	48.2	.008	9.6	0.1	107.6
1956	68.2	43.7	.075	9.1	0.3	102.5
1955	66.1	39.6	.024	8.7	0.3	96.7
1954	62.4	37.3	.035	7.7	0.1	91.9
1953	60.2	33.9	.390	7.2	0.1	86.9
1952	57.3	31.3	.182	7.0	0.8	80.8
1951	54.3	29.4	.219	6.6	. . .	76.9
1950	54.2	28.0	2.619	6.4	1.4	77.0

in interest rates, the relative importance of interest income probably will increase.

In addition to the absolute size of the securities portfolio, investment income also is sensitive to the interest rate environment and the investment strategy followed by the FDIC. This phenomenon first became apparent in the mid-1960s, when market rates started to exhibit some degree of short-term instability.

In the mid-1970s, the FDIC started to pursue an active role in managing its investment portfolio;[6] prior to this time the FDIC

---

[6]The FDIC, except on rare occasions, has not sold securities to take advantage of market conditions. The term "manage" as used in the text refers to investment of cash flows from current income and maturing securities.

	Deposit Insurance Assessments[1]	Investment Income	Other Income	Administrative Expenses	Insurance Losses & Expenses	Net Income
1949	122.7	25.1	.487	6.1	0.3	144.7
1948	119.3	24.8	2.803	6.3[4]	0.7	138.6
1947	114.4	42.9	.455	9.8	0.1	147.6
1946	107.0	23.6	.281	9.9	0.1	120.7
1945	93.7	27.2	.376	9.3	0.1	111.6
1944	80.9	17.8	.784	9.2	0.1	90.0
1943	70.0	16.3	.319	9.6	0.2	76.8
1942	56.5	12.4	.459	9.6	0.5	59.0
1941	51.4	10.6	.018	9.5	0.6	51.9
1940	46.2	9.7	.049	9.4	3.5	43.0
1939	40.7	10.4	.030	9.2	7.2	34.8
1938	38.3	9.4	.012	8.8	2.5	36.4
1937	38.8	9.3	. . .	8.5	3.7	36.0
1936	35.6	8.2	. . .	8.3	2.6	32.9
1935	11.5	9.2	. . .	8.5	2.8	9.5
1934-33	. . . [2]	7.0	. . .	9.8[5]	0.2	(3.0)

[1] For the period from 1950 to 1982, inclusive, figures are net after deducting the portion of net assessment income credited to insured banks pursuant to provisions of the Federal Deposit Insurance Act of 1950, as amended.

[2] Assessments collected from members of the temporary insurance funds which became insured under the permanent plan were credited to their accounts at the termination of the temporary funds and were applied toward payment of subsequent assessments becoming due under the permanent insurance fund, resulting in no income to the Corporation from assessments during the existence of the temporary insurance funds.

[3] Includes net loss on sales of U.S. government securities of $105.6 million in 1976 and $3.6 million in 1978.

[4] For the period 1933-1948, includes interest accrued on capital stock held by the U.S. Treasury and the Federal Reserve Banks.

[5] Net after deducting the portion of expenses and losses charged to banks withdrawing from the temporary insurance funds on June 30, 1934.

had assumed a passive role and, in essence, allowed the Treasury to invest the funds in whatever issues it felt appropriate. About this same time, the FDIC started to shorten the average maturity of its portfolio and generally to achieve a better maturity balance. As the earnings problems faced by mutual savings banks became more apparent, the FDIC sharply reduced the average maturity of its portfolio in anticipation of large cash needs and as a hedge against rising interest rates. While the need for the amount of liquidity originally envisaged never materialized, a highly liquid position, coupled with historically high short-term interest rates, resulted in extraordinarily high earnings from investments and helped to offset unprecedented insurance expenses during 1981 and 1982.

Assessment income has paralleled the growth of deposits in the banking system. The assessment rebate system adopted in 1950 has resulted in a lower level of assessments being retained by the FDIC. In most years since 1950, the FDIC has retained slightly in excess of 40 percent of gross assessment income. In 1981 and 1982, however, the large insurance losses resulted in retention of about 90 percent of gross assessments. Since a sliding scale of rebates was mandated in 1980, the ratio of the fund to insured deposits has remained within the statutory limits and the rebate has remained at 60 percent of net assessment income.

Administrative expenses of the FDIC have grown roughly in proportion to changes in the price level and staffing requirements.[7] The one exception occurred in 1976, when substantial losses ($105.6 million) on sales of securities were realized in connection with the shift in investment strategy mentioned earlier. Normally, gains and losses on securities transactions are considered to be part of interest income; however, this loss (and a smaller loss realized in 1978) was incurred as a result of a change in operating procedures, and it was decided at the time that the loss was more appropriately an operating expense.

Insurance losses and expenses are related to the number and size of banks requiring financial intervention by the FDIC. Periodically, the expected loss to the FDIC from each active closed bank or assisted merger case is revaluated, and adjustments are applied to the appropriate loss reserve and expense accounts. For accounting purposes, the adjustments are combined with current year losses, and the net is charged to insurance expense. This practice can result in a misleading impression, and can compound the difficulties experienced by readers of FDIC financial statements. Perhaps the best example of the magnitude of the distortion that can occur is the insurance loss of $100 million reported by the FDIC in 1974. Essentially this entire amount was attributable to a revision to the expected loss on the United States National Bank (San Diego) failure that had occurred the previous year. Again in 1982, reported losses included a $158 million reduction in losses associated with assisted mergers of mutual savings banks during 1981. The negative losses reported by the FDIC in 1979 and 1980 also were the result of revisions to original cost estimates.

Table 4-2 presents a summary by year of the number and total assets of failed insured banks, and the losses realized by the

---

[7] Staffing of the FDIC is discussed later in this chapter.

FDIC in connection with these failures. Because of the periodic revaluation of loss estimates, the losses reported for accounting purposes (Table 4-1) cannot be traced easily in this table.

Table 4-2.   Insured Bank Failures, 1934-1982* ($ Thousands)

	Total Failures			Deposit Payoffs		Deposit Assumptions	
Year	Number	Assets	Losses	Number	Assets	Number	Assets
1982	42	$11,632,415	$1,069,130	7	$585,418	35	$11,046,997
1981	10	4,859,060	556,698	2	51,019	8	4,808,041
1980	10	236,164	20,960	3	17,832	7	218,332
1979	10	132,988	7,833	3	13,565	7	119,423
1978	7	994,035	5,885	1	1,660	6	992,375
1977	6	232,612	1,160	0	. . .	6	232,612
1976	16	1,039,292	22,514	3	20,530	13	1,018,762
1975	13	419,950	18,695	3	43,145	10	376,805
1974	4	3,822,596	328	0	. . .	4	3,822,596
1973	6	1,309,675	67,597	3	29,208	3	1,280,467
1972	1	22,054	1,226	1	22,054	0	. . .
1971	6	196,520	193	5	86,781	1	109,739
1970	7	62,147	288	4	37,498	3	24,649
1969	9	43,572	82	4	9,879	5	33,693
1968	3	25,154	12	0	. . .	3	25,154
1967	4	11,993	1,010	4	11,993	0	. . .
1966	7	120,646	479	1	832	6	119,814
1965	5	58,751	3,903	3	57,556	2	1,195
1964	7	25,849	911	7	25,849	0	. . .
1963	2	26,179	286	2	26,179	0	. . .
1962	0	. . .	. . .	0	. . .	0	. . .
1961	5	9,820	1,502	5	9,820	0	. . .
1960	1	7,506	. . .	1	7,506	0	. . .
1959	3	2,859	97	3	2,859	0	. . .
1958	4	8,905	28	3	4,429	1	4,476
1957	1	1,253	. . .	1	1,253	0	. . .
1956	2	12,914	213	1	5,202	1	7,712
1955	5	11,986	230	4	5,950	1	6,036
1954	2	1,138	258	0	. . .	2	1,138
1953	2	18,811	. . .	0	. . .	2	18,811
1952	3	2,388	792	0	. . .	3	2,388
1951	2	3,050	. . .	0	. . .	2	3,050
1950	4	4,005	1,385	0	. . .	4	4,005
1949	4	4,886	369	0	. . .	4	4,886
1948	3	10,360	641	0	. . .	3	10,360
1947	5	6,798	59	0	. . .	5	6,798
1946	1	351	. . .	0	. . .	1	351
1945	1	6,392	. . .	0	. . .	1	6,392
1944	2	2,098	40	1	447	1	1,651
1943	5	14,059	123	4	7,382	1	6,677
1942	20	21,756	688	6	1,603	14	20,153
1941	15	34,805	591	8	17,812	7	16,993
1940	43	161,898	3,796	19	7,960	24	153,938
1939	60	181,522	7,152	32	43,933	28	137,589
1938	74	69,518	2,425	50	13,925	24	55,593
1937	75	40,462	3,672	50	19,376	25	21,086
1936	69	31,955	2,333	42	12,989	27	18,966
1935	25	16,023	2,685	24	11,105	1	4,918
1934	9	2,657	207	9	2,657	0	. . .
Total	620	$25,961,827	$1,808,476	319	$1,217,206	301	$24,744,621

* Includes savings banks merged with financial assistance in order to avert failure: three in 1981 and eight in 1982.

65

Another source of distortion arises from the FDIC's past policies with respect to explicit interest charges on funds advanced in connection with insurance operations. The policy has been not to adjust cost estimates to reflect foregone interest, and this has significantly understated reported losses. Beginning in 1983, the FDIC changed its policy so that explicit interest will be factored into all future cost estimates.

The FDIC's practice of not allocating administrative costs to insurance expense also has tended to understate reported losses. In 1984, the FDIC will begin allocating overhead expenses to each failed bank receivership.

The understatement of historical costs notwithstanding, the loss experience of the FDIC has been modest. A majority of failures of insured banks (360) occurred before World War II, resulting in reported losses slightly less than nine percent of assessments collected over this same period. It was not until the mid-1970s that losses again approached and surpassed this level.

The Deposit Insurance Fund

The deposit insurance fund is the net worth of the FDIC, and represents accumulated earnings retained since 1933. In every year except 1947, when the FDIC retired a majority of the capital stock originally issued to the Treasury and Federal Reserve Banks, the fund has increased and was approximately $14.3 billion in mid-1983.

The fund is often compared to various definitions of deposit liabilities in insured banks in an attempt to measure its ability to absorb losses in the banking system. The relationship that probably has received the most attention is the ratio of the fund to total insured deposits. As a practical matter, however, the concept of an aggregate level of insured deposits has little meaning.

Since the mid-1960s, the FDIC has handled most failed banks in a way that all depositors, and indeed all general creditors, have been afforded *de facto* 100 percent insurance.[8] It is only in cases where the FDIC pays off the depositors of a failed bank that the basic insurance limit becomes relevant. However, even in the case of a payoff, many uninsured depositors are either collateralized or have an offset against an outstanding credit. Thus, the ratio of the fund to insured deposits probably represents an underestimate of the exposure of the fund.

---

[8] This topic is addressed more fully in Chapter 5.

Additionally, the measurement of total insured deposits within the system with any precision has become extremely difficult, if not impossible. The complexities in the law pertaining to the definition of deposits, the method of aggregating individual depositors' accounts within a bank for insurance purposes and the increased activity of brokers, who specialize in gathering funds from many individuals and placing them in fully insured deposit accounts, all contribute to measurement problems.

In Table 4-3, the ratios of the fund to both insured and total (domestic) deposits are presented. Although there have been some fluctuations in these ratios, they have remained remarkably stable over time. This is a reflection of the ability of the FDIC to generate sufficient income to cover operating expenses and insurance losses, and to contribute enough to the fund to maintain a stable relationship to deposit liabilities. Even in 1981-1982, years when record losses were absorbed by the FDIC, the fund increased both in absolute terms and in relation to total deposits.

There are several reasons to believe that the historical relationship of the fund to deposits will continue into the future. Market interest rates tend to move with bank deposits. Over the past 25 years, interest rates on three- to five-year Treasury securities have increased at an annual average compound rate of one to one-and-one-half percent less than deposits in the banking system. While this same relationship has not been constant over time, it is probable that the positive correlation will continue into the future. Whatever the shortfall of interest income, retained assessment income is the other source available to stabilize the ratio of the fund to deposits. The magnitude of this income depends importantly on the volume of insurance losses.

In general, losses incurred by the FDIC in connection with failed banks have been modest. From 1934 to 1980, reported losses and insurance expenses accounted for less than five percent of assessment income. The record losses reported in 1981 and 1982, when losses accounted for approximately 74 percent of assessment income, are not expected to continue over any protracted period of time. While future losses may be higher than those experienced through 1980, losses even greater than the more recent levels would have to persist for several years before the ability of the fund to generate substantial income would be compromised. Although 1981 and 1982 cannot be considered to represent a normal period, it must be recognized that the fund grew by about 25 percent during this period despite the enormous losses absorbed by the FDIC.

67

Table 4-3. The Balance Sheet of the FDIC and Deposits in Insured Banks, 1934-1982 ($ Millions)

	U.S. Govt. Securities	All Other Assets	Total Assets[1]	Deposit Insurance Fund (Net Worth)	Total Deposits in Ins. Banks[2]	"Insured" Deposits[2]	Ratio of Total Deposits	Fund to Insured Deposits
1982	$ 13,559.4	$ 1,674.1	$ 15,233.5	$ 13,770.9	$1,544,697	$1,134,221	.89%	1.21%
1981	12,236.3	1,005.3	13,241.7	12,246.1	1,409,322	988,898	.87	1.24
1980	10,720.9	914.7	11,635.6	11,019.5	1,324,463	948,717	.83	1.16
1979	9,636.1	723.2	10,359.3	9,792.7	1,226,943	808,555	.80	1.21
1978	8,373.1	909.5	9,282.6	8,796.0	1,145,835	760,706	.77	1.16
1977	7,267.0	1,195.5	8,462.5	7,992.8	1,050,435	692,533	.76	1.15
1976	6,760.2	1,795.6	8,555.9	7,268.8	941,923	628,263	.77	1.16
1975	6,472.2	1,877.5	8,349.8	6,716.0	875,985	569,101	.77	1.18
1974	5,966.2	2,211.5	8,177.9	6,124.2	833,277	520,309	.73	1.18
1973	5,639.5	283.8	5,923.3	5,615.3	766,509	465,600	.73	1.21
1972	5,333.0	122.6	5,455.6	5,158.7	697,480	419,756	.74	1.23
1971	4,831.0	162.2	4,993.2	4,739.9	610,685	374,568	.78	1.27
1970	4,575.1	56.2	4,631.3	4,379.6	545,198	349,581	.80	1.25
1969	4,261.1	36.3	4,297.4	4,051.1	495,858	313,085	.82	1.29
1968	3,942.9	27.7	3,970.7	3,749.2	491,513	296,701	.76	1.26
1967	3,661.4	30.2	3,691.7	3,485.5	448,709	261,149	.78	1.33
1966	3,413.9	29.2	3,443.2	3,252.0	401,096	234,150	.81	1.39
1965	3,190.2	21.5	3,211.7	3,036.3	377,400	209,690	.80	1.45
1964	2,981.5	27.3	3,008.8	2,844.7	348,981	191,787	.82	1.48
1963	2,798.1	25.0	2,823.1	2,667.9	313,304[3]	177,381	.85	1.50
1962	2,634.8	10.7	2,644.5	2,502.0	297,548[4]	170,210	.84	1.47
1961	2,470.4	11.0	2,481.5	2,353.8	281,304	160,309	.84	1.47
1960	2,324.7	11.9	2,336.6	2,222.2	260,495	149,684	.85	1.48
1959	2,189.5	7.9	2,197.4	2,089.8	247,589	142,131	.84	1.47
1958	2,060.6	6.8	2,067.5	1,965.4	242,445	137,698	.81	1.43
1957	1,944.9	5.9	1,950.9	1,850.5	225,507	127,055	.82	1.46
1956	1,831.2	8.7	1,840.0	1,742.1	219,393	121,008	.79	1.44
1955	1,725.4	8.6	1,734.0	1,639.6	212,226	116,380	.77	1.41
1954	1,628.8	3.8	1,632.7	1,542.7	203,195	110,973	.76	1.39
1953	1,530.5	6.2	1,536.7	1,450.7	193,466	105,610	.75	1.37
1952	1,441.3	2.6	1,444.0	1,363.5	188,142	101,841	.72	1.34
1951	1,356.2	4.0	1,360.3	1,282.2	178,540	96,713	.72	1.33
1950	1,278.3	3.9	1,282.2	1,243.9	167,818	91,359	.74	1.36
1949	1,207.2	4.4	1,211.7	1,203.9	156,786	76,589	.77	1.57
1948	1,066.0	5.9	1,072.0	1,065.9	153,454	75,320	.69	1.42
1947	1,022.5	8.2	1,030.7	1,006.1	154,096	76,254	.65	1.32
1946	1,047.7	13.0	1,060.7	1,058.5	148,458	73,759	.71	1.44
1945	899.9	31.1	931.0	929.2	157,174	67,021	.59	1.39
1944	762.0	44.1	806.2	804.3	134,662	56,398	.60	1.43
1943	573.3	87.5	660.8	703.1	111,650	48,440	.63	1.45
1942	536.8	81.9	618.7	615.9	89,869	32,837	.69	1.88
1941	419.9	104.6	524.6	553.5	71,209	28,249	.78	1.96
1940	384.5	112.6	497.2	496.0	65,288	26,638	.76	1.86
1939	363.5	92.5	456.1	452.7	57,485	24,650	.79	1.84
1938	372.7	48.8	421.6	420.5	50,791	23,121	.83	1.82
1937	348.5	36.8	385.3	383.1	48,228	22,557	.79	1.70
1936	332.6	20.5	353.2	343.4	50,281	22,330	.68	1.54
1935	298.3	38.9	337.2	306.0	45,125	20,158	.68	1.52
1934	315.1	18.4	333.7	291.7	40,060	18,075	.73	1.61

[1] Due to rounding differences, components may not add to totals.

[2] Deposits in foreign branches are omitted from totals. Insured deposits are estimated by applying to the deposits in the various types of accounts at the regular Call dates, the percentages insured as determined from the Summary of Deposits survey submitted by insured banks. Unless otherwise noted, deposits are as of December 31 of each year.

[3] December 20, 1963.

[4] December 28, 1962.

68

The nature of the assessment mechanism is another important reason why the fund-to-deposit relationship can be expected to remain relatively stable over the longer-run. The rebate system in essence places 60 percent of losses directly with insured banks; this provides a cushion to the fund in absorbing insurance losses. Further, if operating expenses and losses exceed gross assessment income, the excess is carried forward to subsequent years and is charged against gross income in the same manner as current losses. Moreover, current law ties the proportion of net assessment income returned to insured banks to the relationship of the fund to insured deposits. Thus, there could be situations where the fund actually declines, but the system would automatically accelerate the rate of income retention until historical relationships have been restored.

Insurance Coverage

Several factors determine the effective insurance coverage afforded individual depositors in an insured bank. First is the basic insurance limit in effect at the time a bank fails. The limit is set by law and currently stands at $100,000. Second, protection can be expanded beyond the basic insurance limit by use of multiple accounts held in different forms of ownership. Finally, and perhaps most importantly, effective coverage depends on the way the FDIC chooses to handle a failed bank.

The basic insurance limit represents the minimum insurance coverage available to a bank depositor. The original limit was set at $2,500 in the 1933 Act, but was increased to $5,000, effective June 30, 1934. This limit remained in effect until 1950, when it was increased to $10,000 as part of the Federal Deposit Insurance Act. The limit was next increased to $15,000 in 1966, to $20,000 in 1969 and to $40,000 in 1974. In 1974, the insurance limit for time and savings accounts held by state and political subdivisions was increased to $100,000; this same limit was extended to Individual Retirement (IRA) and Keogh Accounts in 1978.

The most recent increase occurred in 1980, when it was raised to $100,000 for all types of accounts despite the FDIC's reservations (the FDIC also had resisted previous increases in the insurance limit). This represented a departure from previous changes in insurance coverage, which generally had been more modest and more or less reflected changes in the price level. The increase to $100,000 was not designed to keep pace with inflation. Rather, it was in recognition that many banks and savings and loan associations, facing disintermediation in a high interest rate climate, had sizable amounts of large certificates of deposits (CDs) outstanding. The new limit facilitated retention of some of these deposits or replaced outflows from other deposit accounts with ceiling-free CDs. In 1980, only time accounts with balances of $100,000 or more were exempt from interest rate ceilings.

A depositor may increase insurance coverage by maintaining multiple accounts held in different forms of legal ownership. In determining the insurance coverage afforded a depositor, the statute has always required the FDIC to aggregate all balances held in the same right and capacity before application of the basic insurance limit. Accounts held in different rights and capacities, however, are each insured up to the basic limit.

Until 1967, the FDIC relied on state laws to define what constituted different forms of deposit ownership. Because state laws often differed on this topic, this practice often led to confusion and sometimes hard feelings on the part of depositors in closed banks. In 1967, the FDIC and the Federal Savings and Loan Insurance Corporation (FSLIC) cooperated in an effort to produce regulations that would set forth a consistent set of rules defining how the agencies would treat multiple accounts for insurance purposes. While consistency was achieved, the resulting rules are complex.

One of the unanticipated outgrowths of the way in which insured deposits are defined is the practice of brokers gathering funds in individual amounts up to the basic limit, and purchasing large, fully-insured CDs from banks.[9] Since the funds are held in an agency relationship, each identifiable ownership interest is insured to the basic limit, although balances would be aggregated with other deposits held by owners to determine balances for insurance purposes. This activity accelerated after the payoff of Penn Square Bank in July 1982, as investors (depositors) searched for the highest return without incurring any default risk.

The expansion of insurance coverage through the use of brokers has been of great concern to the federal deposit insurance agencies. Dating from the early debates on deposit insurance legislation, there has been a fear that deposit guarantees would erode the discipline of depositors on the actions of banks.

---

[9]There are other ways the same result can be achieved. For example, some brokers purchase a large CD, and then offer participations in amounts up to the insurance limit to individual investors.

The increased activity of brokers has heightened these concerns, and was the subject of extensive discussion in Congress, the regulatory agencies and the financial community during 1983.

Depositors in some cases also may increase the effective deposit insurance limit by utilizing the right of offset. A depositor has the right to apply outstanding loan balances to reduce the balances in deposit accounts. Since deposit balances for insurance purposes are determined after applicable offsets, otherwise uninsured deposits can be protected by means of this mechanism. In a closed bank situation, the FDIC does not have the right to offset loan balances against deposit accounts unless the credit is carried in a delinquent status. Unless an explict request is made by the debtor/depositor, loan balances are kept intact and the total deposit balances are insured to the basic limit.

During most of the first 30 years of its existence, the FDIC routinely exercised its statutory right to withhold payment of insured deposits until all indebtedness of the depositor to the closed bank had been satisfied. This practice had its beginnings during the period when there were concerns that the deposit insurance fund would not be adequate to handle insurance losses, although the policy continued long after the need for it had passed. Eventually, vocal protests from irate depositors and prodding by some consumer activists persuaded the FDIC to abandon this policy in 1964.

The level of effective deposit insurance coverage becomes relevant only in cases where depositors in a failed bank are paid off to the basic insurance limit. Sometimes the FDIC will handle a failing or failed bank situation by providing direct assistance to the bank or by assisting an open-bank merger with another bank. More often, a failed bank's non-subordinated liabilities will be assumed by another banking organization. The result in these situations is that all depositors and other creditors with equal or preferred standing are afforded the benefits of 100 percent insurance coverage. Although the philosophy governing the handling of troubled banks has changed over time (see Chapter 5), in the past decade most failures, and virtually all large failures, have been handled by assumption transactions. Payoffs have occurred when no interested or qualified purchaser could be found, or where there was evidence that significant unbooked liabilities or contingent claims existed. The latter circumstance normally occurs where the bank fails as a result of fraud or excessive insider abuse. In many cases depositors have been placed in a position of having insurance coverage dependent not only on factors outside their control, but on factors that they could not be reasonably expected to know prior to failure.

In closing this section, it perhaps is appropriate to note that the FDIC has spent considerable time and effort trying to inform the public about federal deposit insurance coverage. Most of this effort has centered on what is and what is not an insured deposit, and what deposit insurance means to a depositor if a bank should fail. Admittedly, the rules are complex, although the basic purpose of deposit insurance seems clear to most people. Evidently, this is not always true. Two examples may serve to illustrate the point.

Ed Johnson, who began work as an FDIC claim agent in 1938, recalled an incident in which a depositor of a failed New Jersey bank appeared unsatisfied with his FDIC check for $225. While admitting this was, in fact, his account balance, the customer indicated a nearby FDIC sign: "But, the sign, she say $5,000."

"I guess," said Johnson, "he thought he hit the jackpot!"[10]

In the second incident, an office of Maryland's Register of Wills received a telephone call in the late 1970s from a recently widowed woman. Her husband had an FDIC-insured bank account, she related, and now that he had died she wanted to know how to collect the $40,000 insurance. Hopefully this was not an integral part of their estate planning.

Organization and Staffing

The first task facing the FDIC was to develop an organization and staff to perform the insurance admission examinations required by the 1933 Act. This task consumed almost all available resources during 1933. By the time the temporary fund began operations on January 1, 1934, virtually all of the examinations had been completed. Attention thus shifted to development of an organization to handle the ongoing responsibilities of the insurance agency. This task was one of the first problems faced by Leo Crowley when he became Chairman in early 1934.

Traditionally, the organization chart of the FDIC has reflected a mixture of functional and specialized responsibilities typical of

---

[10]Interview with Ed Johnson, "Early Claim Agents Had Key Role in Payoff of Insured Deposits," *FDIC News* (August 1983), Vol. 3:9, p. 2.

Chart 4-1. FDIC Organization Chart

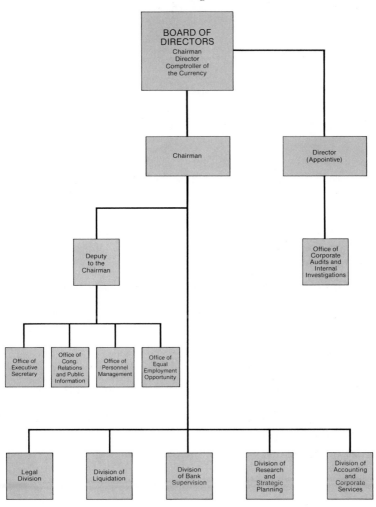

many organizations. The two primary responsibilities of controlling risks to the insurance fund and providing for the orderly liquidation of assets acquired from failed and failing banks were placed in the Division of Examinations (renamed the Division of Bank Supervision in 1969) and the New and Closed Bank Division (renamed the Division of Liquidation in 1936). Other activities, although in some cases acting as an integral part of the bank examination or liquidation functions, have had a separate existence within the corporate structure. Chart 4-1 presents the current organizational structure of the FDIC.

Table 4-4. Total Employment by Function, Selected Years (Year-End)

	Bank Supervision	Liquidation	Legal	Other	Total
1934	592	8	15	231	846
1940	609	998	37	283	1,927
1945	497	342	35	310	1,184
1950	727	90	24	234	1,075
1955	816	58	22	235	1,131
1960	938	38	23	244	1,243
1965	1,078	101	36	231	1,446
1970	1,890	175	54	389	2,508
1975	2,282	423	83	486	3,274
1980	2,544	460	107	533	3,644
1982	2,129	778	105	492	3,504

By federal agency standards, the FDIC has never been a large agency. By the end of 1934, total employment stood at 846, and reached a peak of 3,773 in 1978. Table 4-4 presents total employment for selected years and, where possible, the employment within each functional area. Because of numerous internal reorganizations and shifting responsibilities, it is virtually impossible to reconstruct a consistent employment series for most of the major areas of responsibility.

Except for the period 1939-45, when liquidation activity had intensified because of the large number of bank failures during 1934-40, most of the resources of the FDIC have been devoted to the bank examination process. Historically, employment in the Division of Bank Supervision has averaged about 65 percent of all FDIC personnel. Most of these employees are located in the twelve regional offices situated around the country (see Chart 4-2). The FDIC had originally established fifteen regional offices, but they were cut back to twelve in 1935. In 1966, the number was increased to fourteen, before being reduced to thirteen in 1981 and to the present level in 1983. Within each region there are a number of field offices, located in most of the larger cities, to coordinate on-site examinations.

Employment within the Division of Bank Supervision has depended on the size and complexity of banks directly examined by the FDIC, perceptions of risk within the industry and additional regulatory requirements imposed by Congress. With the exception of the World War II years, and the personnel shortages that accompanied the war effort, the staff of the division slowly and steadily grew through the late 1960s. Beginning at this time, Congress passed a series of laws, primarily in the consumer protection area, that placed additional responsibilities

Chart 4-2. FDIC Regions

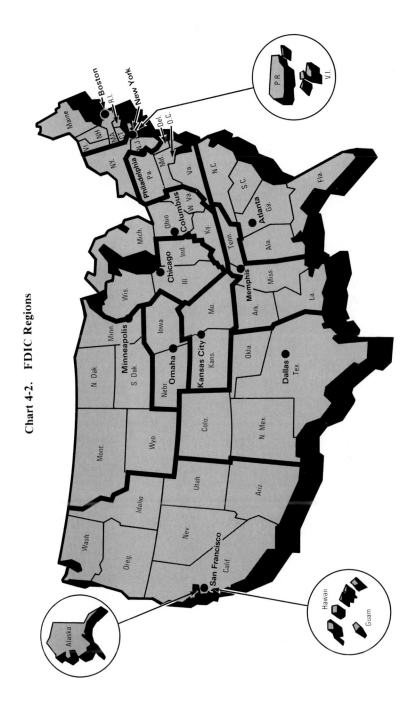

on the regulatory agencies. Additionally, banking had become more complex and, at least by the early 1970s, more exposed to adverse economic conditions. Staffing of the division began to reflect those changes in about 1967; the annual growth rate in employment approximately doubled during the 1967-82 period. Greater emphasis on cost control, accompanied by increased reliance on state examinations and off-site monitoring systems, resulted in a reduction of personnel in the division from a peak of 2,648 in 1978 to 2,129 at the end of 1982.

Although the Division of Liquidation performs a variety of activities, including payment of insured depositors in payoff cases, most of its personnel are engaged in the liquidation of assets acquired from failed banks. Historically, employment has depended on the number of active liquidations and the size and complexity of acquired assets. Employment reached a peak of 1,623 in 1941. While there were only about $130 million in assets being liquidated at that time, there were 286 active liquidations. By way of contrast, there were $2.2 billion in assets and 128 active cases at year-end 1982, and only 778 total employees at that time.

The large number of active liquidations in the 1940s was a result of the relatively large number of bank failures occurring from 1934 to 1942. As these liquidations were terminated and few banks failed over the next 30 years, employment in the division was drastically reduced. The low point was reached in 1952, when there were only 32 people engaged in liquidation activities. Since the early 1960s, the number of employees gradually increased through the early 1970s as a result of a conscious effort to build and retain an experienced staff of liquidation specialists. More recently, the division has grown more rapidly in response to the need to liquidate larger and more complex assets and, in the last two years, in response to an accelerating rate of bank failures. By late 1983, the division employed approximately 1,400 people.

The published number of employees operating in the Division of Liquidation includes both permanent FDIC employees and others who are hired at the liquidation site on a temporary basis. These so-called Liquidation Graded (LG) employees provide to the FDIC a means to fill needs of a temporary nature without having to maintain a very large permanent staff. In times of peak liquidation activity, LG employees normally comprise the majority of the division's employment.

In recent years, the Division of Bank Supervision has provided examiners to the Division of Liquidation on a detail or temporary basis. These examiners are used in the initial period after a bank is closed to assist in inventorying and appraising assets and investigating bond claims, civil claims against officers and directors and criminal matters. In some of the larger, more complex failures, large numbers of examiners have been utilized for these purposes and, in some cases, have been assigned to a liquidation for several months.

In 1981, the division reorganized its operations, effectively decentralizing much of its activities. Prior to this time, administrative services were handled in the Washington office, with liquidation activities performed at sites located in close proximity to the location of failed banks. The reorganization created five area offices to act as regional administrative centers and provide a means to consolidate individual liquidation sites on a more timely basis (see Chart 4-3).

The FDIC's bank supervision and liquidation functions normally require a considerable amount of legal services. This activity traditionally has been performed by a permanent staff of attorneys, supplemented by the use of outside counsel. The internal staff of lawyers always has been organized to provide "open-bank" and "closed-bank" service. Until 1940, the closed-bank operations were organizationally located in the Division of Liquidation; since 1940, virtually all staff attorneys have been assigned to the Legal Division.

Staffing of the Legal Division has been determined by the same factors that have affected other operations of the FDIC. Employment in the open-bank section has reflected the needs of the Division of Bank Supervision and the requirements to promulgate rules and regulations relating to banking activities. On the other hand, employment in the closed-bank section has reflected the number and complexity of bank failures.

In 1967, attorneys were assigned to some regional offices of the Division of Bank Supervision on an experimental basis. This program was successful and was extended to the area offices of the Division of Liquidation during 1983. These attorneys still report directly to the General Counsel, although their work is most directly related to the activities of the remote locations to which they are assigned.

The FDIC always has maintained some form of research capability. The Division of Research historically has served in a

Chart 4-3. FDIC Liquidation Areas

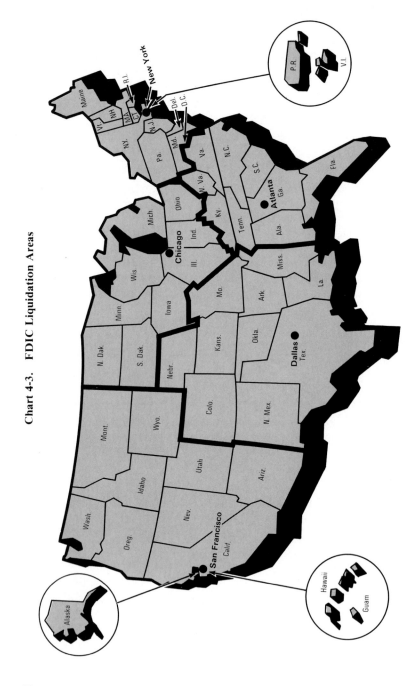

support capacity, particularly in the areas of economic and financial analysis of developments in banking, resolution of problem bank situations and legislative matters. The division also has engaged in longer-term research relating to matters of interest to the FDIC. During most of its existence, the research function was performed in conjunction with the statistical responsibilities of the FDIC.[11] In 1977, research activities were segregated from the statistical function and made a separate operating unit reporting directly to the Chairman. The division's name was changed to the Division of Research and Strategic Planning in 1981, reflecting additional responsibilities. Employees devoted to research have averaged about 30 persons in recent years.

The other activities performed by FDIC employees have been variously assigned to the executive offices (Office of the Chairman) and other operating units. In 1981, the internal structure of the FDIC was reorganized. The accounting, data processing and facilities management activities were placed in the Division of Accounting and Corporate Services. This move combined what had been the comptroller's function with the data processing area. The other support areas were placed either under the Appointive Director (internal audits) or the Deputy to the Chairman (secretariat, congressional relations and public information, personnel and equal employment opportunity). The size of the staffs in each of these areas has grown in proportion to the complexity of FDIC internal operations and the increased demands placed on the agency by the supervision and liquidation functions.

---

[11]Beginning in 1934, the FDIC has collected, edited and published periodic balance sheet and income statement information from FDIC-regulated banks.

Chapter 5
Handling Bank Failures

An important consideration in setting up the FDIC was the establishment of an agency that, in addition to providing deposit insurance, would handle bank failures and liquidate failed bank assets in an orderly, inexpensive and nondisruptive manner. These latter functions have played an important role in the FDIC's 50-year history.

Procedures Used in Handling Failures — Early Years

The Banking Act of 1933 authorized the FDIC to pay up to $2,500 to depositors in insured banks that failed. The only procedure to be used to pay depositors was a Deposit Insurance National Bank (DINB), a new national bank chartered without any capitalization and with limited life and powers. Twenty-four insured banks were placed into receivership and their deposits were paid off through a DINB by the FDIC during the period of the temporary insurance plan, January 1, 1934 to August 23, 1935.

The 1935 Act gave the FDIC authority to pay off depositors directly or through an existing bank, and once that additional authority was granted, the FDIC ceased using the DINB for the next 29 years. During the past 20 years, the FDIC has used a DINB five times, the last occasion being the failure, in 1982, of Penn Square Bank, N.A., in Oklahoma City. The DINB essentially provides a vehicle for a slow and orderly payout, and its use in recent years has been confined to situations where only limited banking services were available in the community or where, as in the case of Penn Square, a regular payoff would have been substantially delayed.

In addition to broadening the ways in which a payoff could be effected, the 1935 Act gave the FDIC the authority to make loans, purchase assets and provide guarantees to facilitate a merger or acquisition. This authority had been sought by the FDIC because of its concern that many of the banks that had been granted insurance might not survive, and paying off insured depositors in these banks would be too expensive. In addition, most banking observers felt that there were too many banks in operation and that it would be desirable if the FDIC could facilitate an orderly reduction in their number through increased mergers.

Between 1935 and 1966, the procedure used by the FDIC to merge out failing banks did not actually involve a pre-merger closing or the establishment of a receivership. Acquiring banks assumed all the deposits of a failing bank and an equivalent amount of assets. In early assumption transactions, the FDIC determined the volume of sound assets of the failing bank and made a demand loan for an amount equal to the difference between deposits and sound assets, the loan being collateralized by the remaining assets. The FDIC would demand payment and foreclose on the remaining assets. Thus, the acquiring bank obtained cash and sound assets equal to assumed deposit liabilities. The FDIC would liquidate the acquired assets and repay itself for its cash advance from these proceeds. If collections exceeded the FDIC's advance plus interest, excess collections went to stockholders of the merged-out bank.

After several years in which loans were used to effect assumption transactions, it became apparent that certain legal problems that complicated the transaction (these related to bank borrowing limits and collateral foreclosure procedures) could be avoided if, instead of lending to the failing bank, the FDIC purchased assets from it. Consequently, direct purchase of assets became the standard procedure for facilitating a merger and the same general result was accomplished.

Beginning in 1935, the FDIC had two options in handling bank failures: payoffs or assumptions. When banks were paid off, depositors received direct payments from the FDIC up to the insurance limit. Uninsured depositors had a claim on the receivership for the uninsured portion of their deposits along with the claims of other general creditors, including the FDIC, which stood in the place of the insured depositors that it had paid.[1] In these transactions uninsured depositors frequently did not receive the full amount of their deposits, and even when they did, there typically were long delays resulting in some loss through foregone interest. In assumption transactions, uninsured as well as fully insured depositors received all of their funds in the form of deposits in the acquiring bank. Once the FDIC began using the assumption transaction, it appears that the decision on which procedure to be used depended primarily on whether a potential, interested acquirer existed. Most payoffs occurred in states that did not permit branching so that an acquisition could not be easily effected.

---

[1] In receiverships prior to August 1935, the FDIC was a preferred creditor and was paid prior to uninsured depositors.

It should be kept in mind that throughout its history the FDIC has not had the authority to close banks. That has rested with the Comptroller of the Currency in the case of national banks and with the state banking authorities in the case of state-chartered banks. Generally, the FDIC has worked closely with the primary supervisor in disposing of failing banks.

FDIC as Receiver

Prior to 1934, national bank liquidations were supervised by the Comptroller of the Currency, who had authority to appoint the receiver and had a permanent staff of bank liquidation specialists. Liquidations of state banks varied considerably from state to state and before 1900 were most often handled under the provisions for general business insolvencies. By 1933, most state banking authorities had at least some control over state bank liquidations.[2] The increased incidence of national bank failures from 1921 through 1932 created a shortage of experienced receivers. Complaints were heard that receiverships, both national and state, had been "doled out as political 'plums', the recipients of which attempt to make as much commission as possible, and to keep the job going as long as possible."[3] There were also conflicting concerns that depositors had to wait too long to recover their funds and that liquidators were causing undue hardship in the community by dumping acquired assets. When the FDIC was established, insured depositors could receive their funds more quickly without requiring rapid asset liquidation.

When a national bank is closed, the FDIC is automatically appointed receiver by the Comptroller of the Currency. When an insured state bank is closed, a receiver is appointed according to state law. In 1934, 30 states had provisions by which the FDIC could be appointed receiver but, in practice, most often it was not. In the first 63 state bank liquidations, the FDIC was named receiver only seven times. Today, however, it is the exception when the FDIC is not appointed.

Before the FDIC can pay off insured depositors certain tasks must be performed. These include: posting and balancing individual deposit accounts up to the day of closing; computing and

---

[2]Cyril B. Upham and Edwin Lamke, *Closed and Distressed Banks—A Study in Public Administration* (Washington, D. C.: The Brookings Institution, 1934), p. 30.

[3]Ibid., p. 62.

On July 5, 1934, Mrs. Lydia Lobsiger received the first federal deposit insurance disbursement, following the failure of the Fond Du Lac State Bank in East Peoria, Illinois.
Photo: UPI

84

crediting interest on deposits up to the closing; merging of deposit accounts where multiple accounts exist to determine insurance liability; separating claims of depositors who have past due obligations to the bank; and preparing checks for payment. In some instances, the determination of precise insurance coverage may be a matter for subsequent litigation.

Every effort is made to begin the payoff as soon as possible, and in many instances the delay is only a few days.[4] Depositors have 18 months in which to establish a claim with the FDIC. Customers whose deposits exceed the limit of coverage become general creditors for the balance due them, except in a few states where depositors are preferred over other creditors.

When the FDIC pays off insured deposits, it becomes a creditor of the receivership for the amount of its advances. Its claims against a receivership arise from its role as an insurer, and it essentially stands in the place of insured depositors. When appointed receiver, the FDIC assumes a fiduciary obligation to all creditors of the receivership and stockholders of the bank, with the responsibility to maximize the amounts recovered for them in as timely a manner as possible. The Federal Deposit Insurance Act, in Section 11(d), requires that liquidations be conducted "having due regard to the condition of credit in the locality." This means that liquidations should be conducted in an orderly manner, avoiding a forced-sale dumping of assets. This requirement not only lessens the impact on the community, it is also conducive to realizing the greatest possible value on recoveries.

As assets of the receivership are liquidated, proceeds are periodically distributed as dividends to creditors, on a *pro rata* basis. If sufficient recoveries are made so that all creditors are fully paid, the remaining assets are turned over to the bank's stockholders. While this has occurred on occasion, the more typical receivership finds that the assets are not sufficient to satisfy all claims. In these instances, the receivership remains in existence until all recoverable assets have been liquidated or until the expected cost of recovery exceeds the value of the remaining assets.

---

[4]It is generally conceded, however, that delays in the case of a large bank payoff could be considerably longer.

Cost Test

Improved economic conditions in the late 1930s and during World War II significantly reduced the number of bank failures. Beginning in the mid-1940s, the FDIC ceased paying off banks. In its 1944 *Annual Report*, the FDIC reviewed disbursements and collections in payoffs and assumption transactions and suggested that the latter were a more efficient means of handling failing banks. Moreover, it suggested that the assumption method "provides a more flexible method of liquidating the affairs of an insolvent bank than does placing it in receivership. Depositors were fully protected; there was no break in banking service . . . and the community does not suffer the economic dislocations which inevitably follow a bank suspension."[5]

There was one payoff in 1944 and none between 1945 and 1953. During this latter period there were 24 assumptions, including cases in Illinois, Missouri, Texas, and Wisconsin — all essentially unit banking states. The FDIC was able to arrange assumption transactions with newly chartered banking groups in several of these cases. In its 1950 *Annual Report*, the FDIC boasted that "for nearly seven years receiverships of insured banks in difficulty have been avoided, and no depositor of any insured bank has lost a single penny because of bank failures. This constitutes an all-time record in the nation's history for bank solvency and safety of deposits."[6]

In Senate hearings on the confirmation of FDIC Directors in the fall of 1951, Senator Fulbright, then presiding subcommittee chairman, questioned the FDIC policy of providing 100 percent *de facto* insurance to banks. While FDIC representatives defended their policies, Senator Fulbright argued that the FDIC was going beyond the scope of the insurance protection that Congress had contemplated and that the FDIC record suggested that its decisions to avoid receiverships did not reflect any substantial analyses or cost calculation.[7] In October 1951, FDIC Chairman Maple Harl wrote to Senator Fulbright and indicated

---

[5]Federal Deposit Insurance Corporation, *Annual Report*, 1944 (1945), p. 18.

[6]Federal Deposit Insurance Corporation, *Annual Report*, 1950 (1951), p. 12.

[7]U.S., Congress, Senate, Committee on Banking and Currency, *Hearings before a subcommittee of the Senate Committee on Banking and Currency on the Nominations of H. Earl Cook and Maple T. Harl to be Members of the Board of Directors of the Federal Deposit Insurance Corporation*, 82d Cong., 1st sess., Part 2, September 27 and October 1, 1951.

that in the future the FDIC would undertake a cost calculation to determine whether an assumption would be cheaper than a payoff. Thereafter, the FDIC began to use a cost test in determining how to handle failing banks, and the prevailing thinking within the FDIC shifted to the opinion that the wording "such action will reduce the risk or avert a threatened loss to the Corporation" in Section 13(e) of the FDI Act required the FDIC to make an explicit cost calculation in deciding to facilitate a merger rather than paying off a bank. This is not a universally held interpretation.[8]

While the legal basis for requiring the cost test may have been in doubt, the FDIC continued to use it during the next 31 years. The Garn-St Germain Depository Institutions Act of 1982, which significantly revised Section 13 of the Federal Deposit Insurance Act, explicitly inserted a cost test.[9]

Closed-Bank Purchase and Assumption Transactions

The FDIC began to shift to payoffs in the 1950s, and between 1955 and 1958 there were nine payoffs and only three assumption transactions. From 1959 through 1964 there were 18 payoffs and no assumptions. By the mid-1960s, the FDIC had rediscovered assumption transactions and it was recognized that there were advantages to having a bank closed by the Comptroller or the state, creating a receivership, and effecting a purchase and assumption transaction out of the receivership. This procedure eliminated the need for stockholder approval and, in certain instances, reduced the potential exposure of the acquiring bank and, indirectly, the FDIC.

In open- and closed-bank transactions the FDIC sometimes had several options with respect to assuming banks, and limited

---

[8]Golembe has argued, "Section 13(e) says nothing at all about a comparison of the use of the deposit assumption techniques with the deposit payoff procedures, nor does it require, in our view, that the former be less costly than the latter. But Senator Fulbright, who must long since have forgotten his little personal feud with the FDIC directors, still exerts his influence over the FDIC decisions!" Carter H. Golembe, *Golembe Reports*, vol. 1974-8: *Memorandum re: Bank Failures and All That* (Washington, D.C.: Carter H. Golembe Associates, Inc., 1974), p. 11.

[9]In connection with revised provisions related to facilitating a merger, the Act states: "No assistance shall be provided . . . in an amount in excess of that . . . necessary to save the cost of liquidating . . . ."

negotiations occurred with respect to such matters as loans to be assumed by the acquiring bank and the valuation of banking premises. However, it was not until January 1966 that the FDIC received an explicit premium in a purchase and assumption transaction, in connection with the failure of Five Points National Bank in Miami, Florida. By 1968 the FDIC had developed an explicit bidding process for handling closed-bank purchase and assumption transactions (P&As), and this was the way most bank failures, including practically all of the larger ones, were handled during the next 15 years.

A bank is closed and a uniform package is offered to bidders. This package consists of deposits and other nonsubordinated liabilities and a like amount of assets, less the amount of the premium bid. In its simplest form the assets consist of bank premises (subject to subsequent appraisal), cash assets, securities valued at market, performing consumer loans and cash furnished by the FDIC to equate acquired assets (less the premium paid) to assumed liabilities.

With the use of an explicit premium, the FDIC established a more formal procedure for its "cost test" and made it more likely that a P&A would be cheaper than a payout. When a bank was closed the FDIC estimated the cost of a payout by determining the shortfall in likely asset collections, the share of nonsubordinated liabilities accounted for by insured deposits and the expense associated with the actual payoff. Since the FDIC made all general creditors whole in a P&A, its share of the likely loss would be increased by the use of a P&A. However, that might be more than offset by the premium bid so that a minimum premium necessary to justify a P&A could be calculated beforehand and compared with the best bid received. In practice, the estimates of likely loss and even the level of insured deposits were not very precise so that there was a considerable margin of error in this calculation.

Using this procedure, the FDIC handled most commercial bank failures and practically all large failures through purchase and assumptions during the next 15 years, except where certain circumstances prevailed. These generally fell into two categories: (1) situations typically in nonbranching states where there was virtually no interest in acquiring the failed bank, and (2) situations where substantial fraud or other factors indicated the likely presence of significant unbooked liabilities or contingencies, which made it difficult to estimate the ultimate loss in the transaction and hence made it difficult to apply the cost test.

Bank Failures Since 1970

The early 1970s were relatively prosperous and there were only 17 bank failures between 1971 and 1974. Nevertheless, they included the first comparatively large failures encountered by the FDIC. Banking was becoming more competitive and the economic environment was becoming less forgiving. The first oil price shock occurred in 1973 and contributed to a rising inflation rate and new highs in interest rates in 1974.

The severity of the 1973-1975 and the 1981-1982 recessions led to a sharp increase in commercial bank loan losses and an increase in the number of bank failures. The 1973-1975 recession led to substantial real estate loan problems. In many instances these persisted well beyond the onset of economic recovery and, as a result, the bank failure rate remained high, peaking in 1976 at 16, the highest number since 1940.

The 1981-1982 recession was severe and it followed a weak recovery. The economy experienced its worst performance of the post-World War II period from the standpoint of unemployment, capacity utilization and business failures, and in 1982 there were 42 bank failures, including eight mutual savings banks. Despite the turnaround in the economy during the first half of 1983, there were still 27 bank failures during this period.

The first $100 million-plus failure handled by the FDIC was the $109 million Birmingham Bloomfield Bank (1971), located in a Detroit suburb. That bank was affiliated with the same management group whose policies brought the billion dollar Bank of the Commonwealth in Detroit to the brink of failure. Both institutions had invested heavily in long-term municipal bonds, relying considerably on purchased deposits, in anticipation of expected interest rate declines. When interest rates rose, the institutions incurred losses and found themselves locked into low-yielding, depreciated securities. The experience of these institutions did not prevent other banks from subsequently getting into situations where they became vulnerable to high and rising interest rates. To some extent that problem existed for the Franklin National Bank, which failed in 1974, and the First Pennsylvania Bank, N.A., which received financial assistance from the FDIC in 1980.

When interest rates rose dramatically in 1979-1980 and again in 1981-1982, most FDIC-insured mutual savings banks found themselves locked into long-term, low-yield assets (primarily mortgages) while their deposit costs rose substantially. Most incurred operating losses, and in 1981 and 1982 a total of 11 mutual savings banks failed. Throughout the FDIC's history, there have been 25 failures of commercial banks with assets over $100 million, all of which occurred since 1971. All but one of these failures were handled by purchase and assumption transactions. (This excludes the three surviving $100 million-plus banks that received financial assistance to avert failure. See Table 5-1.)

Large Bank P&As

While the handling of smaller bank failures has tended to become routine, those involving larger banks have frequently

Table 5-1. Twenty-Five Largest Banks Requiring FDIC Disbursements ($ Millions)

Rank	Name/Location	Date	Assets	Action[1]
1.	First Pennsylvania Bank, N.A. Philadelphia, PA	4/80	$7,953	13(c)
2.	Franklin National Bank New York City, NY	10/74	3,656	P&A
3.	New York Bank for Savings New York City, NY	3/82	3,403	FAM
4.	Greenwich Savings Bank New York City, NY	11/81	2,491	FAM
5.	Dry Dock Savings Bank[2] New York City, NY	2/83	2,452	FAM
6.	Western Savings Fund Society Philadelphia, PA	1/82	2,113	FAM
7.	First National Bank of Midland Midland, TX	10/83	1,547	P&A
8.	Union Dime Savings Bank New York City, NY	12/81	1,365	FAM
9.	United States National Bank San Diego, CA	10/73	1,266	P&A
10.	Bank of the Commonwealth Detroit, MI	1/72	1,257	13(c)
11.	Western New York Savings Bank Buffalo, NY	1/82	1,022	FAM
12.	Farmers & Mechanics Savings Bank Minneapolis, MN	2/82	980	FAM
13.	Central Savings Bank New York City, NY	12/81	899	FAM

involved special circumstances and sometimes included bidding situations that were tailored for the specific case. In October 1973, the $1.3 billion United States National Bank (USNB) in San Diego became the first billion dollar failure, and it was followed, in 1974, by the failure of the Franklin National Bank in New York, the country's 20th largest bank, with assets of about $3.6 billion. Both of these failures involved special problems. USNB had outstanding a substantial volume of standby letters of credit that the FDIC sought to isolate from the transaction by considering them contingent claims with lesser creditor standing than depositors, and hence the FDIC. Holders of

Rank	Name/Location	Date	Assets	Action[1]
14.	United Mutual Savings Bank New York City, NY	12/81	833	FAM
15.	United American Bank Knoxville, TN	2/83	760	FAM
16.	Banco Credito y Ahorro Ponce, PR	3/78	713	P&A
17.	Fidelity Mutual Savings Bank Spokane, WA	3/82	689	FAM
18.	United States Savings Bank Newark, NJ	3/82	675	FAM
19.	Penn Square Bank, N.A. Oklahoma City, OK	7/82	517	Payoff
20.	Abilene National Bank Abilene, TX	8/82	446	FAM
21.	Hamilton National Bank Chattanooga, TN	2/76	412	P&A
22.	Farmers Bank of the State of Del. Wilmington, DE	6/76	370	13(c)
23.	American City Bank Los Angeles, CA	2/83	319	P&A
24.	Oregon Mutual Savings Bank Portland, OR	8/83	266	FAM
25.	City & County Bank of Knox County Knoxville, TN	5/83	262	P&A

[1] 13(c): financial assistance from the FDIC to avert failure.
FAM: financially assisted merger of a failing but open bank.
P&A: financially assisted merger of a failed (closed) bank.
Payoff: payment of insured deposits in a failed bank.
[2] Merger was voluntary but with FDIC financial assistance.

standby letters of credit of USNB sued the FDIC and won,[10] the court decision coming almost five years after the bank failure.[11] The FDIC could not discriminate against equivalent classes of creditors, and in this case the court ruled that the claimants in question had general creditor status. This case meant the FDIC would have to take account of contingent claims in applying the cost test to determine whether to pay off a bank or use a P&A. Contingent claims might include — in addition to standby letters of credit — outstanding lawsuits and claims arising from loan participations and failure to meet loan commitments. Since it is frequently difficult to assess liability on such claims at the time of a bank failure, additional uncertainty was injected into the decision process and influenced subsequent behavior of the FDIC.

The Franklin failure absorbed a substantial amount of FDIC personnel resources. There were negotiations over a five-month period among the FDIC, the Comptroller of the Currency, the Federal Reserve and the bidding banks. The transaction was complicated by the presence of foreign branches and foreign exchange speculation. As negotiations went on, Franklin experienced an enormous deposit outflow, which was funded by advances from the Federal Reserve Bank of New York. In the P&A transaction that was worked out, the winning bidder was required to take assets of Franklin equal to the remaining deposit liabilities less the premium bid. The trust activities of Franklin were sold separately to another institution. In contrast, the P&A bidding on USNB had been relatively simple. The FDIC agreed to remove the substantial volume of loans linked to that bank's management, and the transaction was effected quickly without significant deposit outflows.

By the time Franklin was closed, its borrowings from the Federal Reserve had reached $1.7 billion. The FDIC agreed to pay the amount due the Federal Reserve in three years, with periodic payments to be made from liquidation collections. The Federal Reserve released the collateral it held in connection with Franklin's borrowings. The FDIC had paid the Federal Reserve note down to about $600 million at the end of three years and, when it repaid the New York Fed in 1977, that represented the first significant cash outlay by the FDIC in that transaction.

---

[10] *First Empire Bank, New York, et al.* vs *FDIC*, 572 F.2d 1361 (9th Cir.), cert. den. 431 U.S. 919 (1978).

[11] It appears that the FDIC anticipated an unfavorable decision on this case several years earlier and this seems to have entered into cost calculations.

Subsequently, the FDIC recovered its cash outlay plus interest from additional liquidation collections.

The manner in which the Franklin P&A was handled significantly reduced the volume of assets to be liquidated by the FDIC. In several other large bank failures the FDIC sought to limit the volume of assets it took back by requiring winning bidders to take unclassified loans subject to certain limited buy-back arrangements. In smaller P&As, particularly where bidders were given little time to evaluate the condition of the failing bank, bidders generally received a "clean" bank. The winning bidder in the Franklin transaction was European-American Bank, a New York-chartered bank that was much smaller than Franklin, but a subsidiary of several very large European banks. In several subsequent P&A transactions, the FDIC invited foreign banks or subsidiaries of foreign banks to bid and in a few instances they were the winning bidder.

In two subsequent P&As, the FDIC accepted winning bids that involved two or more banks dividing up assets and liabilities of failing banks. These occurred in the case of Banco Credito in Puerto Rico in 1978 and American City Bank in California in 1983.

Bids received by the FDIC on failed banks have depended on the attractiveness of the franchise of the failing bank and its deposit mix, state branching laws and other considerations. An internal study done by the FDIC sought to explain the relationship between winning bids received by the FDIC and the volume of acquired deposits. Generally the explanatory variables were: (1) the volume of core deposits, essentially demand deposits and retail time and savings deposits (little value was given to large CDs and public deposits); (2) the number of bids submitted; (3) the attractiveness of bank franchises generally as measured by price-earnings ratios of bank stocks or the relationship between bank stock prices and book value; (4) the level of short-term interest rates (reflecting the fact that the FDIC typically provided a substantial volume of cash); and (5) the size relationship between the winning bidder and the bank acquired, a reflection of the likelihood that relative size of an acquisition is a good measure of the riskiness of the acquisition.

Until July 1982, every bank failure involving assets greater than $100 million had been handled through a P&A transaction. The largest payout was the Sharpstown State Bank in Houston, Texas, which failed in 1971 and had deposits of $67 million in

27,000 accounts. Litigation related to that bank's failure persuaded the FDIC that it could not reasonably assess the likely cost of a P&A transaction. Large bank failures were handled through P&As because that appeared to be the cheaper course. However, in most cases, precise cost calculations were difficult to make and close cases were probably resolved on the side of a P&A for several reasons. P&As were less disruptive to the local community and to financial markets generally. Moreover, the mechanical problems (balancing records, working out offsets and paying checks) of paying off a large bank with tens or hundreds of thousands of deposit accounts could conceivably take a month or longer.

Open-Bank Assistance

In 1950, the FDIC sought legislation to provide assistance to banks, through loans or the purchase of assets, to prevent their failure. Apparently there was concern that the Federal Reserve would not be a dependable lender to banks faced with temporary funding problems, particularly nonmember banks. The Federal Reserve opposed this recommendaton, considering it an infringement on its lender-of-last-resort function. Congress did give the FDIC authority to provide assistance to an open bank, but it imposed restrictive language related to the circumstances under which such assistance could be given. Section 13(c) permitted such assistance "when in the opinion of the Board of Directors the continued operation of such bank is essential to provide adequate banking service in the community."

The FDIC did not use the authority of Section 13(c) until 1971, and it has only been used a total of five times. On one occasion (1974), open-bank assistance was given to provide temporary funding in order to buy time to arrange a P&A of American Bank & Trust (AB&T) in Orangeburg, South Carolina.[12] This assistance was justified by the fact that AB&T was the only source of banking services in ten of the communities in which it operated, although other banks were located in nearby communities. It appears that this assistance could have been provided under Section 13(e), which allows the FDIC to provide financial assistance to facilitate the absorption of a failed or failing bank without a finding of "essentiality." AB&T was acquired by another bank 12 days after the assistance was given.

---

[12]The Federal Reserve had declined to lend to AB&T, a $150 million nonmember bank. In 1980 the availability of the Federal Reserve discount window to nonmember banks was made explicit by Congress.

On the other four occasions that Section 13(c) was utilized by the FDIC, it was intended that the recipient bank would remain open and independent. Unity Bank and Trust Company in Boston (1971) and Bank of the Commonwealth in Detroit (1972) both served inner-city neighborhoods that were otherwise lacking adequate banking services. Farmers Bank of the State of Delaware (1976) was partially owned by the state and was its sole depository. The FDIC found the services provided by these three banks to be essential to at least a portion of the communities they served. In the most recent use of Section 13(c), assistance was given to First Pennsylvania Bank, N.A., in Philadelphia (1980). With assets of nearly $8 billion, First Pennsylvania was the city's largest bank, and its failure would have been the largest in U.S. history. In this case, the FDIC's determination of "essentiality" was based mainly on the bank's size. It would have been difficult to arrange a P&A, and the closing of such a large bank would have had serious repercussions not only in the local market but probably nationwide as well. This reasoning was also a factor in the "essentiality" finding for Bank of the Commonwealth, which had assets of $1.3 billion. In the Unity Bank and First Pennsylvania cases, other banks were partners to the assistance plan, agreeing to supply credit up to a certain amount. In the case of Farmers Bank, the State of Delaware joined the FDIC in aiding the bank.

Today, of the five 13(c) assistance cases, only First Pennsylvania has survived with the same ownership. Bank of the Commonwealth and Farmers Bank were sold but remain open, and AB&T and Unity Bank eventually failed.

The FDIC's authority under Section 13(c) was expanded by the Garn-St Germain Depository Institutions Act of 1982. At the discretion of its board of directors, the FDIC may provide necessary assistance to prevent the failure of any insured bank. Only if the cost of assistance would exceed the cost of closing and liquidating the bank does the FDIC have to make a finding of "essentiality." It is anticipated that the authorization of 13(c) assistance will continue to be the exception, though. The FDIC remains reluctant to use Section 13(c) because of its concern that the assistance would benefit stockholders, materially erode market discipline and keep afloat a weakened bank to the possible detriment of the local community.

As problem situations have become larger and more complex, the FDIC has been more inclined recently to make temporary loans under Section 13(e). This assistance provides the time

American Banker

Friday, November 6, 1981

Greenwich Rescue May Top All in Cost

By KAREN SLATER and LAURA GROSS

NEW YORK — If the price tag for this week's assisted takeover of the Greenwich Savings Bank is inde~ $465 million the Feder~ surance Corp ~ will ~

Tuesday, July 6, 1982

THE DAILY OKLAHOMAN

Penn Square Bank Declared Inso|

THE WALL STREET JOURNAL
Wednesday, July 7, 1982

Penn Square's Failure Bodes Losses for Many

FDIC Can't Arrange Merger To Protect Creditors, Uninsured Depositors

By G. CHRISTIAN HILL
Staff Reporter of THE WALL STREET JOURNAL
OKLAHOMA CITY—For the first time in ~ numbers of uninsured de~ ~tors stand to lose money in ~

THE WALL STREET JOURNAL, Friday, October 19, 1973

Rescue Mission

Big San Diego Bank Is Insolvent; Sale Is Set; Depositors Protected; Shareholders to Lose

THE NEW YORK TIMES, SUNDAY, FEBRUAR~

A 'Problem' Bank Goes Under

Hamilton National's Failure Was 3d Largest

By FRED TRAVIS

NASHVILLE — Two weeks ago the Comptroller of the Currency, James E. Smith, told a Senate committee that there were seven national banks in "immediate" danger of collapse. Now there are

THE TREND OF BANK FAILURES
In billions of dollars

Includes Franklin National Bank

Includes U.S. National Bank

Deposits of Failed Banks

Number of Failures

'55 '56 '57 '58 '59 '60 '61 '62 '63 '64 '65 '66 '67 '68 '69 '70 '71

Source: Federal Deposit Insurance Corporation

$1.8

FRANKLIN FOUND INSOLVENT BY U.S. AND TAKEN OVER

European Group in Control After Biggest Bank Failure
—Depositors Protected

By JOHN H. ALLAN
The Franklin National Bank was declared insolvent yesterday in the largest bank failure in American banking history. The institution was immediately taken over by the European-American Bank and Trust Company, a New York State-chartered entity owned by six of the largest banks in Europe. All depositors of the Frank~ lin will be~

necessary in the most difficult circumstances to arrange a P&A and minimizes disruption in the local market. Also, 13(e) advances can be secured, are short-term and do not require a finding of "essentiality." Temporary, subordinated loans of $25 million and $100 million were provided in 1983 under 13(e) to the United Southern Bank, Nashville, Tennessee, and the First National Bank of Midland, Texas, to provide time to work out an acceptable P&A for each bank. Also in 1983, a commitment was made to loan $250 million to Seattle First National Bank on a short-term, subordinated basis under Section 13(e). The bank was purchased by BankAmerica Corporation without FDIC assistance, so the 13(e) line was never utilized.

Penn Square Bank

During the July 4th weekend in 1982, the Comptroller of the Currency closed the Penn Square Bank, N.A., in Oklahoma City, with deposits of $470 million, and the FDIC set up a DINB to pay off insured depositors. Penn Square had been an aggressive lender principally to small oil and gas producers. It had grown rapidly, relying heavily on purchased deposits and, to a much greater extent, on a program of participating the loans it originated to large regional and money center banks. As a result, when the bank failed it was servicing a loan volume almost five times the bank's liabilities. The loans were premised on extremely high oil and gas prices, and when the market weakened and production was curtailed, they went into default, and what collateral supported them had only limited value.

The FDIC paid off Penn Square primarily because it was not possible to assess the likely cost of alternatively arranging a P&A. Due to the heavy volume of loan participations and questions about the accuracy of information furnished to loan purchasers, a substantial volume of lawsuits was anticipated (and, in fact, have been filed). If those suits are successful, the cost to the FDIC of a P&A transaction would ultimately have been very substantial. By paying off insured depositors, the FDIC's maximum loss was the $250 million in insured deposits. This amount actually will be reduced by the FDIC's share of receivership collections. Had a P&A been effected, the FDIC would have had to agree to protect any acquiring bank from unbooked and contingent liabilities. To the extent that these were established in court, the FDIC would have had to pay full value on these claims. The way the failure was actually handled, claims established from lawsuits will have status in the receivership equal to other general creditors, including the FDIC.

The FDIC Board believed that the case for a payoff, as against a P&A, was overwhelming and that the FDIC would lose all credibility if it effected a P&A in the Penn Square case.[13] That would have given financial markets a signal that all deposits, at least in banks above a certain size, were, for all practical purposes, fully insured. Discipline in the markets would have been seriously eroded, with deleterious long-term ramifications. Paying off Penn Square, though, had immediate repercussions. Uninsured depositors became more sensitive to the possibility of loss and could not assume that all but the smallest bank failures would be handled through purchase and assumption transactions. Some banks had difficulty rolling over large CDs. The business of brokers, who divide up large deposits and participate them to several banks, was significantly boosted. Depositors generally became more selective in their choice of banks, and the public's concern about the condition of banks was increased.

Recent Open-Bank Assumption Transactions

In the fall of 1982, the FDIC entered into two transactions where acquisitions of failing commercial banks were facilitated without the closing of these banks. These were essentially assisted mergers, but in each case (Abilene National Bank, Texas, and Oklahoma National Bank and Trust Company) the stock of the failed bank had been pledged as collateral to the acquiring institution. The stock was foreclosed, a merger was effected and the FDIC provided assistance. Stockholders of the failed bank obtained virtually no benefit from the transactions. In one instance the FDIC lent money on favorable terms to facilitate the transaction and in the other case the FDIC agreed to buy back loss loans when they surpassed a specified level. In both cases the FDIC Board believed that these transactions would be considerably cheaper than a payoff or a closed bank P&A. Other important considerations were that FDIC liquidation resources were considerably stretched at that time and the transactions (particularly Abilene) would not utilize any liquidation staff. At that time, banking in the southwest was still affected by the

---

[13]The presence of a large volume of uninsured deposits in the bank and indications that liabilities substantially exceeded likely asset collections made it extremely unlikely that a P&A could have been cost-justified even if lawsuits were ignored.

uncertainties from the Penn Square failure and additional failures could have had negative repercussions. While the initiative in both transactions came from the acquiring institutions, the FDIC went back to the pre-1966 procedure in working out negotiated pre-failure mergers of failing commercial banks. However, in both of these cases, special circumstances related to stock ownership helped make the transactions feasible for the FDIC in that shareholders received no subsidy and claims against officers, directors and others were preserved.

Assisted Mergers of Mutual Savings Banks

Mutual savings banks had been vulnerable to rising interest rates for several decades. Most of their asset portfolios consisted of long-term, fixed-rate assets, principally mortgages and mortgage-backed securities. An accelerating inflation rate in 1978 and a shift in the manner in which monetary policy was conducted in the following year led to an almost continuous rise in interest rates until the spring of 1980. Despite a sharp, though brief, break in interest rates in 1980 and a smaller decline in the fall of 1981, interest rates remained near record levels through mid-1982.

During this period interest ceilings on time deposits were raised several times and a variety of new deposit instruments were made available to banks and thrifts. Nevertheless, substantial amounts of deposits shifted from banks and thrifts to money market funds or to market securities, and depository institutions experienced both disintermediation and an increased cost of funds.

At the same time, yields on savings bank asset portfolios changed very little because of their lengthy maturities, and as the cost of funds rose, earnings disappeared and losses began to grow. By early 1982, aggregate savings bank losses were running at about a $2 billion annual rate, about 1.25 percent of assets. However, some of the weaker institutions in New York City were losing at a rate of 3.5 percent of assets. The problem faced by the FDIC from the standpoint of potential exposure of the deposit insurance fund was very different from any faced earlier in its history. Asset quality was not a problem. However, in the case of many large institutions that faced "book" insolvency, the market value of their assets was actually 25 to 30 percent below outstanding liabilities. Their failure could have resulted in enormous FDIC losses. The first failing savings bank

99

transaction, involving the $2.5 billion Greenwich Savings Bank in New York, had an initial estimated cost of $465 million, more than the reported cost of handling all previous insured bank failures.

The FDIC's principal concern was how to keep the cost of handling failing savings banks at a reasonable level without undermining confidence in the industry or in the FDIC. Various devices were used to handle failures. One of the most successful was the income maintenance agreement. The FDIC agreed to pay an acquiring institution the difference between the yield on acquired earning assets (primarily mortgages and taxable bonds) and the average cost of funds to savings banks for some number of future years.[14] This might be supplemented by an additional dollar payment in the future or by an up-front cash payment. The income maintenance was subsequently modified so that the FDIC defined the asset base according to existing asset maturities and yields on the failing bank assets and specified prepayment assumptions. Bidding banks would be paid the spread between defined asset yields and the cost of funds, whether they held the failed bank's assets or sold them.

The income maintenance covered any negative interest spread for acquiring banks regardless of what happened to interest rates and the cost of funds. Thus, the FDIC took the interest rate risk on the transactions. The FDIC was in a better position to assume this risk and potential acquirers were willing to bid more aggressively as a result of this. Income maintenance was used in nine of the 12 assisted mergers of failing savings banks between 1981 and early 1983.

The first savings bank transaction was handled through a mixture of bid and negotiation. In subsequent transactions, the FDIC defined certain bidding ground rules and indicated, generally, how bids would be priced, and then entertained bids in a variety of forms. This was in contrast to the way most commercial bank P&As had been handled, where everything was specified beforehand and bidding banks submitted a single number.

Failing savings banks were not actually closed. The transactions were assisted mergers. However, the FDIC insisted that

---

[14]Previously, the FSLIC had provided assistance along these general lines in connection with an assisted interstate merger. The FDIC's assistance to Bank of New Orleans in the closed-bank P&A of International City Bank in 1976 had also contained characteristics similar to the income maintenance agreement.

100

senior management and most trustees could not serve with the surviving institution. Since there are no stockholders in mutual institutions, the FDIC did not have to concern itself with receivership interests of existing stockholders. In several of the failing savings banks there were subordinated notes that normally would have only a claim on the receivership in a purchase and assumption transaction on a closed bank. Generally, the FDIC negotiated with noteholders, forcing them to take a lower interest rate and/or an extended maturity. Thus, noteholders took a substantial "hit". In pursuing this policy the FDIC weighed the cost of not wiping out noteholders altogether, by closing the bank, against offsetting considerations. These included possible lawsuits to delay the transactions, greater flexibility for the acquiring institution in continuing leases and other contractual arrangements, cooperation from state supervisors and the possible impact on deposit outflows in other savings banks.

Two of the acquiring institutions were commercial banks and the remainder were other savings banks. Most of the latter were losing money at the time the transactions were effected, although they tended to be stronger than most of their peers. Traditionally, the FDIC has been reluctant to solicit bids from poorly performing institutions, but during this period stronger commercial banks were reluctant to bid aggressively on savings banks because of the asset depreciation and its impact on their balance sheets, and because of the potential impact on capital ratios. In order to keep its cost down the FDIC was willing to compromise on bidder standards and acknowledged the possibility, at least within the agency, that in an unfavorable interest rate environment, some of the acquiring banks could encounter difficulty in the future.

For the most part, classified assets were relatively unimportant in the failing savings banks, and after the first few transactions, when some problem assets were removed, virtually all assets were passed to the acquiring bank. As a result, the cost of the transactions was determined at the outset where FDIC assistance was confined to cash or notes, or else costs were dependent principally on future interest rate developments. Where the latter was the case, future costs were estimated by discounting projected future payments based on prevailing interest rates. The present value of estimated outlays was immediately determined. When interest rates subsequently declined, loss estimates were adjusted to reflect actual outlays and revised future outlays. Between the fall of 1981 and the end of 1982, there were 11 assisted savings bank mergers. The assets of the failing institutions totaled almost $15 billion, more than the total assets of all failed commercial banks since the FDIC was founded. Based on cost of funds projections made at the end of 1982, the cost of these transactions amounted to about 10 percent of assets. While this appears to be a higher cost than typical commercial bank failures, comparative figures may be deceiving. Until 1983 the FDIC did not take account of forgone interest in calculating its losses in commercial bank failures. If adjustment is made for this, then the cost of the savings bank transactions appears to be no higher than the relative cost of most commercial bank failures.

The Garn-St Germain Bill, which was passed in October 1982, included provisions, despite FDIC reservations, whereby savings banks and other qualifying institutions could apply for net worth certificates if they met certain conditions with respect to losses and low surplus ratios. In December 1982, the FDIC implemented a program enabling savings banks to apply for these certificates in amounts equal to a percentage of operating losses. The certificates count as surplus for regulatory purposes. The certificates involve essentially a paper exchange, enabling the institutions to continue to operate. By mid-1983, 24 savings banks with assets of about $37 billion were utilizing this program, and they had approximately $300 million in net worth certificates outstanding. The decline in interest rates has cut savings bank losses, increasing the possibility that many of these institutions will be able to survive or else be merged out with only limited assistance. The net worth certificate program has forestalled savings bank failures, at least temporarily. During the first half of 1983, there was only one assisted savings bank merger, and that was essentially a voluntary transaction that could have been forestalled through the use of net worth certificates.

FDIC Liquidation Activity

The two goals of a receiver — liquidating assets as quickly as possible and realizing the greatest possible value — can come into conflict because sometimes it is desirable to hold an asset until market conditions improve. An obvious problem, though, is that poor asset quality is a factor in virtually every bank failure, and liquidating assets is normally a very lengthy procedure.

102

In its first seven years of operation, the FDIC handled an average of 50 failures annually. As a result, the failure-related assets acquired by the FDIC increased, peaking at $136 million in 1940. Over the next three decades, failures averaged fewer than four annually, but these were generally larger banks than had failed in the early years. Still, the volume of assets in liquidation, which was only $2 million in 1952, did not again reach the 1940 level until 1971. FDIC liquidation activity has escalated dramatically in the past decade. The volume of assets in liquidation reached $2.6 billion in 1974, and stood at $2.2 billion at the end of 1982, and $4.3 billion by December of 1983. Through November of 1983, the FDIC had been involved in 665 receiverships, of which 170 were still active.

Receivers of failed banks always acquire some loans which are in default. These result in litigation and, when secured, foreclosure on collateral. Many failed banks have been involved in what might euphemistically be referred to as "atypical" financial dealings, and the FDIC's liquidation portfolio has, from time to time during the past 50 years, included some rather unusual assets. In one instance, a bank failed because its president was illegally diverting bank funds to finance production of a motion picture. The failure occurred after filming had been completed but before editing. The FDIC then had to decide whether the movie, which had some name actors but was hardly an Academy Award threat, was likely to return the additional investment required to complete and distribute it.

The FDIC has also had interests in oil tankers, shrimp boats and tuna boats and has experienced many of the pitfalls facing the maritime industry. An oil tanker ran aground, a shrimp boat was blown by a hurricane onto the main street of Aransas Pass, Texas, and the tuna boats were idled when the price of tuna dropped sharply. Other liquidation assets have included several taxi cab fleets; a coal mine that was on fire the day the bank was closed; a horse training facility, two inept race horses and quarter horses valued at several million dollars; thousands of art objects, including an antique copy of the Koran; a collection of stuffed wild animals; and all forms of real estate, including churches and synagogues. Single bank failures have resulted in the FDIC's acquisition of 400 single-family homes and as much as $500 million in international loans. Assets have also included loans secured by distribution rights to a well known blue movie ("The Happy Hooker"), by the operation of a house of prostitution and by the warehouse inventory of a "King of Pornography."

103

Assets require active FDIC management when, for one reason or another, their sale cannot be arranged quickly. This can necessitate additional investment by the FDIC, as well as development or acquisition of highly specialized expertise. Asset management has required purchasing wind machines to protect citrus orchards from freezing weather as well as beehives for pollination of almond trees. The FDIC's mortgage interest in a Chicago meat warehouse was abandoned when the refrigeration system failed, and one million pounds of meat spoiled. FDIC liquidators have been called upon to operate hotels, motels, condominiums, office buildings, restaurants, a bakery and a kennel. One management problem involved a residential real estate development, an attraction of which was a golf course that happened to be located in a flood plain (providing some insight into the developer's acumen). An investment of $1 million was required to improve the golf course and thereby enhance the overall marketability of the development. The FDIC also found itself in possession of an abandoned gold mine in Idaho. A buyer could not be found until the FDIC had transformed the property into a successful tourist attraction.

As predecessor to the FDIC's Division of Liquidation, the New and Closed Bank Division supervised seven receiverships in 1935 with a staff of 25 employees. It was also involved with 26 other liquidations for which the FDIC had not been appointed receiver but was a major creditor by virtue of having paid insured deposits. The personnel requirements of the Division have fluctuated widely from year to year, dictated by the number, size, complexity and duration of active receiverships. In the early 1940s, the Division employed more than half of all FDIC personnel, topping 1,600 in 1942, having had to handle nearly 400 failures from the time that deposit insurance became effective in 1934. In the early 1950s, by comparison, as few as 32 liquidation personnel were required as the number of failures had declined in the post-World War II period. Today, because of the recent increase in bank failures and a surge in the volume of assets in liquidation, the Division employs approximately 1,400 people, supplemented by scores of bank examiners on detail from the Division of Bank Supervision.

The occurrence of several bank failures within a short period of time — or even a single large bank failure — can create a sudden demand for experienced liquidators. Some personnel are retained from the failed bank, and many other clerical personnel are hired locally on a temporary basis. The FDIC also relies more heavily now on locally hired liquidation specialists to assist its professional staff.

Present Liquidation Procedures

When a bank is closed by its supervisor and the FDIC is appointed receiver, the first task is to take custody of the bank premises and all records, loans and other assets of the bank. In some instances, even this initial task has been formidable. Franklin National Bank in New York, for example, operated 108 branch offices, and its closing required a force of 778 FDIC personnel, most of whom were examiners on temporary assignment from the Division of Bank Supervision. When The First National Bank in Humboldt, Iowa was closed in 1982, weather conditions conspired to make it all but impossible for FDIC personnel to reach the bank. After first dodging tornadoes, they were confronted by a severe snowstorm that turned expected journeys of only a few hours into two-day ordeals. Happily, serious injuries were avoided, but these employees endured highway closings, vehicle abandonments and numerous accidents, completing portions of their trip by tractor trailer and state police car. That same weekend, in addition to monitoring these travails in Iowa, FDIC officials in Washington had to arrange the mergers of a failing $2 billion savings bank in Philadelphia and a small bank in Virginia, for which no buyer could be found until nearly midnight on Sunday (occasioning what may have been the latest FDIC board meeting).

Sometimes a banker is unwilling to accept his bank's insolvency. In an incident in Indiana, the president of a bank about to be closed had moved a cot into his office, threatening first not to leave and later to commit suicide. The situation was resolved peacefully.[15]

After possession of the bank has been taken, notices are posted to explain the action to the public. Locks and combinations are changed as soon as possible, and correspondent banks and other appropriate parties are notified of the closing by telephone and telegram. In a payoff all incoming debit items, such as checks, are returned marked "drawee bank closed." Deposits received after the closing are returned in full to the depositors.

---

[15]Interview with Neil Greensides, former Chief, Division of Examinations, "FDIC Pioneer Recalls 'Early Days'," *FDIC News* (June 1983), Vol. 3:7, p. 4.

A Liquidator-in-Charge is appointed by the FDIC to supervise the receivership. To provide some continuity, "non-tainted" employees of the failed bank are hired by the receivership for as long as their services are required. As soon as possible, the liquidation activities are moved to nearby office space rented for that purpose, because in most instances the bank's premises are transferred to another banking organization. Thus, the FDIC has active liquidation offices scattered across the United States and its possessions. The five recently established Area Offices will enable earlier closing of on-site offices because the final stages of liquidations can be handled more efficiently on a consolidated basis. At the end of November 1983, all but 35 of the 170 active receiverships had been consolidated.

The time it takes to conclude a liquidation varies greatly according to the number and size of acquired assets as well as their salability. Markets can readily be found for most loans, which are often sold in blocks; but some assets, particularly those acquired in foreclosure, are more difficult to dispose of for reasonable value. Large bank failures occurring in the past decade have created receiverships so large and complex that some may take ten years or more to complete. The FDIC can serve as a lender-of-last-resort if additional investment is required to protect the interests of the receivership. Whenever possible, though, borrowers are required to establish new banking relationships.

The FDIC is usually quite successful in recovering the disbursements it has made. In the 495 insured bank liquidations that have been completed since 1933, the FDIC recovered about 93 percent of its outlays, faring somewhat better in deposit assumptions (95 percent) than deposit payoffs (89 percent), but in the 170 active cases, recoveries are expected to be lower. The historical recovery rates, however, do not fully take into account the foregone interest earnings on advances to receiverships. This interest was collected only on occasion, after disbursements had been fully recovered. Had this expense been acknowledged, and FDIC advances reduced by the present value of collections, it was estimated that for the period 1934-1980, insurance losses and expenses would have increased from four percent of failed bank assets to nine percent.[16] Beginning in

---

[16]Federal Deposit Insurance Corporation, *Deposit Insurance in a Changing Environment* (Washington, D. C.: Federal Deposit Insurance Corporation, April 15, 1983), p. V-6.

1983, the FDIC's recovery and loss experience will more accurately reflect its money cost.

Until the 1970s, FDIC receiverships generally retained long-term performing assets. This tended to improve reported liquidation results since both interest and principal collections were included in recovery calculations. In recent years the practice has been to sell those assets (*e.g.*, securities, mortgages) that are marketable without concern about boosting "apparent performance." In some cases, holding performing assets has benefited junior creditors and stockholders at the expense of the deposit insurance fund. Even where returns on assets exceed the FDIC's opportunity rate, FDIC policy has opted for early sale, recognizing that the FDIC is not an investment company and that its own investment portfolio is restricted to Treasury securities.

Summary

During its 50-year history the FDIC has handled bank failures by paying off insured depositors or merging the bank on an open- or closed-bank basis. In a small number of cases until the net worth certificate program was implemented, the FDIC has forestalled failures by assisting open banks. The specific manner in which failing banks have been handled has varied according to legislation, the experience gained by the FDIC and the specific nature of the problems faced. When confronted with major problems where traditional approaches may not have worked, the FDIC has been flexible and sometimes imaginative.

Throughout its history certain conflicts have emerged. Periodically the FDIC has had to question whether it is appropriate to raise *de facto* insurance coverage through P&As and assisted mergers when that approach is cheaper or less disruptive, and whether there is a cost associated with providing too much *de facto* insurance. When a bank is going to fail it is desirable to get the transaction done quickly. This argues for simple, clean P&As where P&As are appropriate. However, that means the FDIC must collect on more loans, a result that, in the long run, may be more disruptive to the community and more expensive.

A precisely defined bid situation where bidders submit a single number seems most fair, at least on the surface, and it exposes the FDIC to the least criticism. On the other hand, requiring everyone to bid on the same basis is not always likely to give rise to the best or cheapest solution, and it may favor a particular set of bidders. The FDIC may prefer an absolute ban on helping stockholders or subordinated creditors in assisted mergers or open-bank assistance. However, that may mean foregoing transactions that can save the FDIC a lot of money or forestall other failures. Concern on the part of the FDIC that acquiring banks not be exposed to excessive risk or that they meet certain capital standards or treat goodwill in a particular way can also increase the cost of transactions to the FDIC.

These and other conflicts have been faced by the FDIC during its history and have not always been resolved in the same manner by FDIC Boards. They will likely continue to confront future FDIC Boards.

Chapter 6
Bank Examination and Supervision

Banking in the United States today is probably more decentralized yet more closely regulated than in any other nation. Each of the approximately 15,000 banks in the United States is examined on a regular basis by at least one federal or state bank regulatory agency. On the federal level, the Office of the Comptroller of the Currency, the Federal Reserve, and the FDIC are, respectively, responsible for the examination and supervision of national, state member and insured nonmember banks. State banks are also examined and supervised by a state bank regulatory agency.

In addition to bank safety and soundness examinations, these agencies carry out compliance, electronic data processing and trust examinations and conduct numerous other supervisory functions as well as collecting and processing financial data. The system in place today has grown and evolved considerably from its modest beginnings in the early 1800s.

Historical Overview

In the early 1800s, banks were usually required to submit occasional financial reports to the state legislature or some other authority so that it could be determined whether they were operating within the powers of their charters. Actual examinations were undertaken only when suspicions were aroused. Even then, however, the examinations were quite superficial and generally ineffective because adequate enforcement powers were lacking.

Other reasons for state supervision related to the taxation of bank profits, state ownership of bank stock and the note-issuing role of state banks. In addition to the states' financial interests in bank operations, there developed concern that bank failures could adversely affect other banks and the public as a whole and that small depositors, in particular, could not adequately assess their exposure.

The New York Safety Fund was created in 1829, and in addition to being the first deposit insurance system, it was the basis for the present system of regular bank examination. Bank supervision, in connection with this fund as well as the others that followed, was more effective than previous attempts because the members of these generally small mutual organizations had a direct stake in minimizing losses. Thus, member bankers were not likely to overlook the misdeeds of a fellow member and were somewhat more appreciative of the role of supervision.[1] As these funds expired, though, so did their supervisory structures.

Federal bank supervision began in 1863 when national banks were authorized under the National Currency Act (which became the National Bank Act in 1864). The newly formed Office of the Comptroller of the Currency was empowered to supervise national banks and was generally credited with more effective supervision than were the state supervisory systems. A majority of banks soon became subject to the more stringent federal supervision since the taxation of state bank notes caused many banks to switch from state to federal charters. By the late 1800s, when the state banking systems had rebounded, the overall quality of state bank supervision was significantly improved. In 1863, there had been only five states that examined banks regularly; however, by 1914 every state performed this function.[2]

Despite improvements in the overall quality of bank supervision, intermittent high rates of failure continued. These failures often resulted in contractions in credit and the money supply, which prolonged recovery from recessionary periods. In 1913, as a response to this problem, the Federal Reserve System was created. State banks were given the option of Federal Reserve membership, which permitted for the first time direct federal supervision of state banks. Thus, by year-end 1913 the "special" nature of banking had resulted in a regulatory apparatus that included two federal agencies as well as the state supervisory systems. This situation was particularly noteworthy given that government regulation of business generally was extremely limited. Initially, however, the Federal Reserve was more concerned with its responsibilities as central bank, and it was not until the 1930s that it regularly exercised its bank examination rights.

Apparently the political compromise that led to the creation of the FDIC did not permit taking any supervisory authority away from existing federal or state agencies, so in 1933 the

[1]Golembe, "Origins of Deposit Insurance," p. 116.

[2]Benjamin J. Klebaner, *Commercial Banking in the United States: A History* (Hinsdale, Illinois: The Dryden Press, 1974), p. 89.

FDIC became the third federal bank regulatory agency, responsible for some 6,800 insured state nonmember banks. The agency also had more limited regulatory responsibility relating to its role as insurer of national and state member banks. In addition to the supervisory goals of the other federal and state banking agencies, the FDIC had the more clearly defined goal of minimizing the risk of loss to the deposit insurance fund.

The financial debacle of the 1930s and the cautious atmosphere that subsequently characterized banking and the regulatory environment importantly influenced FDIC examination policies during its first several decades. Bank examiners continued to review bank balance sheets in a comprehensive manner, focusing particular attention on problem loan situations even when their potential impact on the insurance fund was likely to be minimal. During the first 15 years following World War II, the economy was relatively strong, loan losses were modest and bank failures were rare. In more recent years, though, bank competition began to increase, and so too did the exposure of the insurance fund. The analysis of individual loans became secondary to assessment of the risk exposure associated with overall bank loan and investment policies.

Today, the frequency of FDIC examinations, particularly for better performing, well-managed banks, has been reduced, and greater reliance is placed on the analysis of financial reports submitted by banks. Resources are now more heavily allocated to dealing with existing and potential problem bank situations. While part of the supervisory role of the FDIC relates to overseeing bank activities to ascertain compliance with the law, the principal purpose continues to be to assess the solvency of insured banks to better protect insured depositors and guarantee the continued solvency of the deposit insurance fund.[3]

Admission Examinations

The standards that were established for initial admission into the deposit insurance system were quite lenient relative to those that were to be applied in subsequent years. In order to be certified by the Secretary of the Treasury and thus qualify for in-

[3]The American Assembly conference on *The Future of American Financial Services Institutions* in 1983 included in its recommendations the statement, "The insurer should have the right to protect its interest by such means as examining and supervising the institution, requiring it to maintain a specified amount of capital . . . . The supervisory authority should rest only in the insurer." (p.8).

surance, a state nonmember bank had to present a certificate of solvency from its state supervisor, and the FDIC had to find that the current value of the bank's assets were at least equal to its liabilities. In other words, banks with unimpaired capital of zero or more were eligible for insurance. This lenient approach was in obvious recognition of the unstable condition of the banking industry and was necessary if the FDIC was to be successful in helping to reestablish public confidence in the industry. Too strict a qualifying standard would probably have prompted more failures by accelerating deposit outflows from those banks least able to withstand them. In fact, 10 percent of the state nonmember banks granted insurance had no capital funds.

Although the initial qualifying standard was quite straightforward, a heavy commitment of resources was necessary in order to evaluate the condition of each of the numerous banks applying for deposit insurance coverage. Bank examination consumed nearly all of the FDIC's efforts in the months prior to the establishment of the temporary fund on January 1, 1934. National banks (of which there were 5,061) and state banks that were members of the Federal Reserve System (802) were already being examined on an ongoing basis by their respective federal regulators and, upon certification by the Secretary of the Treasury, were automatically accepted for deposit insurance. State-chartered nonmembers, however, had to apply for insured status, and by the end of 1933 about 85 percent of these banks had done so. The FDIC, therefore, was faced with the rather prodigious task of examining 7,834 banks within a three-month period.

The Division of Examinations was created on October 1, 1933, and sought adequate permanent and temporary personnel from a variety of sources. Examiners from the Office of the Comptroller of the Currency and from the various state supervisory departments were transferred or loaned to the FDIC. Experienced bankers and others with previous examiner experience were also recruited. Field offices were established in 47 cities around the nation, mostly located in state supervisory offices or in offices of the Reconstruction Finance Corporation. At its peak in December of 1933, this temporary force contained nearly 1,700 examiners and 900 other field office support personnel.

The task of completing these admission examinations was largely accomplished as intended by the end of 1933. Of the 7,834 applicant nonmember banks, 83 percent were approved for insurance, 12 percent were rejected, four percent were still pending decisions and less than one percent remained to be examined. Virtually all of the 977 banks that were rejected were found to have liabilities exceeding their assets and were thus technically insolvent. The FDIC set up a special department to work with these banks to help them correct the impairments that prohibited admission to the fund. The corrective efforts included: (1) raising local funds, (2) director's guarantees, (3) purchase by local interests of bad assets and (4) investment in capital obligations by the RFC. The efforts were quite successful and, within a short period of time, only 140 of these banks were unable to qualify for insurance.

National and state member banks were admitted for insurance provided they were certified by the Secretary of the Treasury. In late 1933 the RFC was actively supplying capital funds to these banks (as well as to nonmembers), but as the year came to a close it was apparent that as many as 2,000 banks did not merit certification. President Roosevelt had told the nation that "the banking capital structure will be built up by the government to the point that the banks will be in sound condition when the insurance goes into effect."[4] Jesse Jones of the RFC was afraid that if it were disclosed that 2,000 banks were still unsound, public confidence would be severely undermined. Therefore, he arranged with Secretary Morgenthau to certify these banks in exchange for a promise from the RFC that they would be made sound within the following six months. In all, the RFC supplied $1.35 billion in bank capital during late 1933 and early 1934.

Capital Rehabilitation

After the initial admission examinations had been completed, the Division of Examinations dismantled its temporary examination force. By the end of 1934, field offices had been reduced from 47 to 15 and field office personnel had declined from nearly 2,600 to about 600, including 450 examiners. In early 1934, the FDIC shifted the emphasis of its examination function from determining minimal acceptability to the strengthening of weaker banks, particularly in the area of capital adequacy.

It was determined that minimal safety required banks to have net sound capital equal to at least 10 percent of deposits. Net sound capital was defined as equity, capital notes, debentures

---

[4]Jesse H. Jones, *Fifty Billion Dollars: My Thirteen Years with the RFC, 1933-1945* (New York: The Macmillan Company, 1951), pp. 28-30.

and reserves, less assets classified as worthless or of doubtful value, including bond depreciation. Based upon admission examination findings, all banks not meeting this standard were reexamined during the first six months of 1934.

Of the state nonmember banks admitted to the fund, 35 percent were found to be undercapitalized. Subsequent examinations and rehabilitative efforts reduced this ratio to just 13 percent by the end of 1934. Many other banks recorded significant improvements though they still fell short of the 10 percent standard. For example, 20 percent of the initial applicants had net sound capital of less than five percent, but by year-end 1934 only three percent were under this level.

The same cooperation accorded to banks initially rejected for deposit insurance was given to those insured banks requiring capital rehabilitation. During 1934, insured nonmember banks wrote off adversely classified assets equal to 20 percent of their total capital, but total capital increased by more than eight percent. The RFC supplied most of the funds used to offset these write-offs, while the remainder was supplied by local interests and earnings retention.

By the end of 1934, the concept of federal deposit insurance was generally accepted, even by many of its former detractors. As one measure that public confidence had been restored in the banking system, bank runs were no longer a significant problem, although they did not disappear altogether. Local concerns about the solvency of an individual bank still gave rise to occasional bank runs. In some instances, fears were aroused when it was felt that bank examiners had overstayed their "normal" visit to a bank, although these concerns were usually groundless.[5]

Safety and Soundness Examination Policy

After completing its first two examination tasks — admissions and capital rehabilitation — the FDIC again shifted its examination focus and concentrated on developing permanent examination policies and procedures. The purposes of these examinations were fivefold:

1. appraise assets in order to determine net worth;
2. determine asset quality;
3. identify practices which could lead to financial difficulties;
4. appraise bank management; and
5. identify irregularities and violations of law.

---

[5]Interview with Neil Greensides (former Chief, Division of Examinations), Washington, D.C., August 16, 1983.

In addition to completing and reviewing its own examinations, in 1936 the FDIC began reviewing examination reports of national and state member banks because the FDIC had insurance exposure for these banks supervised by the Comptroller of the Currency and the Federal Reserve.

Some analysts came to the conclusion that supervisory policies in the 1930s were unduly harsh, and that recessionary periods were not the proper time to pressure banks to sell depreciated assets and reduce risk. Such a practice, it was felt, would lead to a restriction of credit as well as otherwise unnecessary bank liquidations or forced mergers. These concerns had been expressed to the Comptroller of the Currency in 1931, but policy directives at that time were generally ineffective.

A sharp recession had begun in 1937, rekindling these criticisms of bank examination policy, and in 1938 Secretary Morgenthau called for a conference of federal bank regulators. This time around, policy changes were strictly translated into examination procedures, resulting in more lenient asset valuation techniques. It was agreed that most bonds would be appraised at book value rather than market value, a policy believed to be more reflective of long-term investment quality. Moreover, a larger proportion of classified assets were to be included in the capital ratio computation. These policy shifts caused only a slight increase in aggregate capital/asset ratios (12.8 percent under the new method versus 12.6 percent under the old), but the difference at individual banks, particularly marginal performers, could be critical.

The 1938 Conference also led to a revision in the nomenclature of asset classification, establishing the four groups which have remained essentially unchanged: (I) not mentioned, (II) substantial and unreasonable risk, (III) loss is probable and (IV) uncollectible (immediate charge-off). Since 1949, categories II, III, and IV have been referred to respectively as substandard, doubtful, and loss.

Impact of World War II. The participation by the United States in World War II affected both the FDIC and the state banks that it supervised, and some of these effects carried on well past the 1940s. The short-term effects included such things as moving some headquarters' personnel to Chicago to vacate Washington office space for the war effort. The FDIC also suffered the same personnel shortage felt by many government agencies resulting from military enlistments and transfers to defense-oriented programs. A shortage of examiners meant that

Leo T. Crowley served as FDIC Chairman from 1934 to 1945. He had previously headed Wisconsin's Banking Review Board, which handled problem bank situations.

the FDIC was unable to fulfill its policy of annual bank examinations. Even after the war, government hiring restrictions and rapid growth in the economy led to a shortfall of qualified examiners, and it was not until 1951 that the FDIC was again able to examine all of its banks annually.

Another temporary effect of the war effort was the transfer to the FDIC of responsibility for the supervision and examination of about 4,000 federal credit unions, though the FDIC did not insure their deposits. Federal credit unions had previously been supervised by the Farm Credit Administration. In 1948, after six years of FDIC supervision, this responsibility was transferred to the Federal Security Agency.

FDIC Chairman Leo Crowley had come to be regarded by President Roosevelt as one of the best administrators, in or out of government, and he accepted numerous wartime responsibilities. While retaining his FDIC post, Mr. Crowley held nine separate government positions, including those of Alien Property Custodian and head of the Foreign Economic Administration, the latter a Cabinet-level post that included the lend-lease program. Thus, all foreign economic dealings, and assets and authorizations totaling more than $40 billion were administered from Mr. Crowley's FDIC office in the Press Building on Fifteenth Street. His ability as an administrator was typified by the fact that, despite his varied and awesome wartime responsibilities, Mr. Crowley invariably concluded his workday at 5 p.m. One evening each week was reserved for a poker game that included Jesse Jones of the RFC and the Ambassador from Brazil.

A more lasting effect of the war was a rapid decline in bank capital ratios, which had been on a downward trend for more than 50 years. However, the same process that led to rapid bank expansion — government financing — reduced the riskiness of bank investment portfolios. By the end of 1944, cash and U.S. government obligations had grown to 79 percent of bank assets. Between 1934 and year-end 1944, the capital/asset ratio of banks had declined from 13.2 to 5.9 percent. Despite the decline in capital ratios, bank examiners were not particularly critical of bank behavior due to the quality and liquidity of bank assets.

Post-World War II Supervision. At the end of 1946, bank loans comprised only 16 percent of assets. However, lending increased steadily, reaching 40 percent in the mid-1950s and 50 percent by the early 1960s. Throughout this period loan losses remained relatively small. Net charge-offs averaged considerably less than one-tenth of one percent of outstanding loans during the 1950s (see Table 6-1). As a result, no more than five banks failed in any year. Bank supervision, which was based on policies and procedures rooted in the banking crises and economic chaos of the 1930s, probably was overly conservative in the relatively prosperous 1950s and early 1960s. Bank lending had increased, but banks were still operating within traditional markets, and risks to the soundness of the banking system as well as to the deposit insurance fund were minimal, even during recessionary periods. Bank failures that did occur often received a great deal of attention, including Congressional hearings in some instances. This concern was reflected in the strict supervisory posture that prevailed during this period, but most bankers were content to accept tight regulation in exchange for the restraints it placed upon competition among banks and with nonbank financial institutions.

In the 1960s, banking began to diversify in a number of different ways. Branching accelerated, new liability instruments were developed and investments were broadened — facilitated by the development of holding companies, secondary markets and more widespread loan participations and purchases. Intensified competition and higher costs of funds put pressure on interest margins, and greater risks were assumed in order to increase portfolio yields. Banks in general, and large banks in particular, had become more susceptible to the effects of business downturns (as reflected in loan loss rates) and interest rate fluctuations. Beginning in 1973, the size and number of bank failures began to increase. The 1973-1975 recession resulted in sharply increased loan losses in 1975 and 1976.

The demands on bank supervision had increased, and it was becoming increasingly difficult to effect adequate supervision (risk assessment and reduction of excessive risk) within the confines of policies and procedures designed for the less diversified, less dynamic industry of previous decades. Edward Roddy, who served as the Director of the Division of Bank Supervision from 1971 until his death in 1975, was credited by many as having been particularly aware of the changes that were taking place in the 1960s and 1970s and of the growing inadequacy of existing supervisory policies. It was largely through his efforts that policies were overhauled in the early and mid-1970s, the first substantive changes in several decades.

Table 6-1. Loan Loss Experience of Commercial Banking Industry, 1950-1982

Year	Gross Loan Charge-Offs ($ Millions)	Gross Loan Loss Rate (%)[1]	Net Loan Loss Rate (%)[2]
1950	80.7	.1656	.0589
1951	85.7	.1516	.0614
1952	88.2	.1418	.0558
1953*	121.0	.1807	.0881
1954*	118.8	.1704	.0637
1955	116.6	.1460	.0619
1956	155.5	.1730	.1024
1957*	143.5	.1526	.0760
1958*	152.5	.1545	.0618
1959	147.8	.1355	.0490
1960*	300.2	.2524	.1735
1961	280.7	.2267	.1535
1962	268.9	.1959	.1217
1963	353.1	.2301	.1553
1964	426.6	.2463	.1452
1965	465.7	.2338	.1624
1966	576.9	.2625	.1899
1967	629.5	.2675	.1897
1968	654.9	.2513	.1625
1969	697.9	.2473	.1732
1970*	1,237.0	.4235	.3360
1971	1,404.5	.4412	.3415
1972	1,251.0	.3380	.2397
1973	1,548.0	.3481	.2607
1974*	2,418.3	.4245	.3435
1975*	3,790.2	.6548	.5602
1976	4,190.6	.6763	.5653
1977	3,607.2	.5103	.3955
1978	3,575.9	.4365	.3054
1979	3,771.3	.4077	.2782
1980*	4,888.1	.4916	.3629
1981*	5,320.7	.4842	.3445
1982*	8,152.7	.6894	.5546

* Denotes a predominantly recessionary year.
[1] The ratio of actual gross losses (charge-offs) to the volume of average gross loans.
[2] The ratio of net losses (gross losses − recoveries) to the volume of average gross loans.

In an important shift in FDIC policy, it was decided that smaller, sound, well-managed banks did not require annual full-scope examinations and that it would be preferable to concentrate examination resources on those banks presenting greater risk to the insurance fund. Banks of any size with known supervisory or financial difficulties would continue to be examined at least once a year. Banks with assets exceeding $100 million would have one full-scope examination in every 18-month period, with no more than 24 months between examinations. Banks under $100 million would undergo alternating full-scope and modified examinations, also once in every 18-month period with no more than 24 months between examinations. The modified examinations were to focus on areas of greatest exposure and on management policies and their effectiveness rather than on asset verification and appraisal.

In more recent years, an increased reliance on examination reports of other agencies and off-site monitoring have permitted FDIC examination schedules to be lengthened further. In 1983, the maximum permissible examination interval for the soundest banks was extended to 36 months, with one visitation or off-site review in each 12-month period in which the bank is not examined. Marginally unsatisfactory banks are examined at least once every 18 months with a visitation or review every six months. Banks with known serious problems continue to be examined annually, with visitations at least every three months. Bank size is no longer an overriding factor, but in all cases the Regional Director retains considerable discretion to order more frequent or thorough examinations.

Examination Procedures. While bank supervision policy changes have been relatively few, examination procedures have undergone frequent change, dictated primarily by the growth of branch banking, bank portfolio shifts and diversification. The number of banks insured by the FDIC has remained remarkably constant, generally between 14,000 and 15,000, but the number of branch offices has grown from about 3,000 in 1934 to over 41,000 today. For many years, all bank branches were examined annually, at the same time as the main office. More recently, both the frequency and scope of most branch examinations have been reduced, a situation made possible by automated and centralized record keeping at most multi-office banks.

Until recently, most examinations relied upon a "surprise" factor to reduce the likelihood that anyone in the bank would be able to cover up illegal practices. Examiners would appear without prior notice at the opening or close of business to examine bank records on an "as is" basis. Because a banker might have had sympathetic friends throughout the town who might warn him about an impending examination, examiners sometimes stayed in a nearby town or registered in hotels under a fabricated company name. Today, banks are often notified by the FDIC of an impending examination so that the bank can assemble the needed records. Obviously this is not the procedure when supervisory suspicions have been aroused or when a bank is in danger of failing (although frequent contacts are maintained in the latter situation). There have also been cases that required concurrent examinations of affiliated banks, most recently in early 1983 that resulted in the closing of several Tennessee banks.

Compliance, EDP and Trust Examinations and Other Supervisory Functions

The complexity of laws and regulations under which banks must operate increases the difficulty of the part of the examination that verifies a bank's compliance with these laws. In fact, in 1977 the FDIC separated much of this function from the basic safety and soundness examination, and compliance examinations are now conducted for this sole purpose. The responsibility of the compliance examiner is to enforce the consumer and civil rights statutes affecting state nonmember banks. These statutes include: the Truth in Lending Act, the Fair Credit Reporting Act, the Fair Housing Act, the Community Reinvestment Act, the Home Mortgage Disclosure Act, the Fair Debt Collection Practices Act, the Electronic Funds Transfer Act and the Equal Credit Opportunity Act.[6]

The problems addressed by these Acts are significant, but the solutions have often been reflective of the political, judicial or popular opinion that can change considerably over time. What is initially viewed favorably as strict enforcement may soon be interpreted as overregulation. Moreover, while the federal bank regulatory system might provide a convenient conduit for the enforcement of many consumer and civil rights statutes, it is possible that there are other more appropriate enforcing agencies

---

[6]A more thorough discussion of consumer legislation enforcement may be found in the FDIC's 1977 *Annual Report*, pages 25-27.

for these laws, which reflect concerns that are only marginally within the purview of bank supervision.

If technological development, primarily in the use of computers, has been a catalyst for bank growth and diversification, so has it aided examiners in developing procedures to keep pace with a changing industry. As the cost of electronic data processing (EDP) systems has declined, even smaller banks have found computers affordable. Banks that choose not to own their own computer system invariably purchase these services from other banks or non-bank suppliers. As with compliance, the FDIC now undertakes separate EDP examinations. As banks have become more reliant upon computers, the potential for computer-based theft or embezzlement has increased at least as much. EDP examinations focus on the adequacy of internal controls and physical security. The federal bank regulators perform joint or alternating examinations of data centers that service banks supervised by different agencies.

As early as 1935, the FDIC organized and trained specialized trust department examiners. Trust department examinations are also separated from regular safety and soundness examinations, though they are usually conducted concurrently.

The FDIC also is responsible for reviewing a variety of applications from insured nonmembers. These include applications for new branches, changes of office location and retirement of capital. Beginning in 1964, these banks had to notify the FDIC if they underwent a change of control (ownership), and in 1978 the FDIC was given authority to deny such a change. The Bank Merger Act of 1960 gave the FDIC the authority to approve or disapprove mergers in which the surviving institution would be under its supervision. In recent years, authority to approve applications for insurance, branches and some mergers has been delegated to the Regional Directors, reducing both the amount of required FDIC resources and processing time. The application forms also have been streamlined and require considerably less information.

Enforcement Powers

Bank examinations frequently uncover situations or practices that are unsafe or even illegal. Except in those instances that require criminal prosecution, the FDIC has several options available to rectify the situation: informal discussions, memoranda of understanding, cease-and-desist orders and termination of insurance.

Following each examination and at other times as needed, examiners meet with bank officials to discuss any problems which were noted during the examination. These informal discussions, often referred to as "jawboning," are usually successful in resolving minor infractions.

For banks found to be in marginally unsatisfactory condition, the FDIC requires written assurance from the bank that specific actions will be taken by the bank to correct its shortcomings. These agreements are referred to as memoranda of understanding (MOUs). They are still viewed as voluntary compliance by the banks but represent the final step before formal enforcement proceedings are begun.

For state nonmember banks found to be in unsatisfactory condition (or others which refuse to enter into an MOU), the FDIC can issue cease-and-desist orders to correct specific situations. A thirty-day notice is given and a hearing is set in the interim. If the order becomes effective and the violations persist, the FDIC may then go to federal court to obtain an injunction. The FDIC also has the authority to issue temporary cease-and-desist orders in the most severe situations. These orders become effective immediately and are made permanent only after the bank has had an opportunity for a hearing. Cease-and-desist orders were authorized by Congress in 1966, but it was not until 1971 that the FDIC issued its first order. The effectiveness of these orders was soon realized, though, and they have been used substantially more frequently in recent years. Because of an increase in problem banks and an aggressive approach to enforcement actions, a record 69 cease-and-desist orders were issued in 1982, and this number was equaled during the first half of 1983.

During its first twenty months of operation, the FDIC had no enforcement authority available to it other than "toothless" coercion of offending bankers, many of whom were opposed both to the concept of deposit insurance and to additional regulation. The Banking Act of 1935 gave the FDIC the authority to terminate a bank's insured status, and this remained the FDIC's sole enforcement authority until cease-and-desist powers were granted in 1966. However, in order to avoid this ultimate sanction, procedures were established to give any offending bank ample opportunity to correct its infractions. If a solution could not be agreed to during informal discussions, the FDIC would then notify the bank's primary supervisor (state or federal), and the bank had 120 days (or less, if so decreed by the supervisor) to correct the problem. At the end of this period, the bank would be reexamined. If the problem persisted, thirty-day notice of insurance termination was given and a hearing date set in the interim. Unless the hearing uncovered contradictory evidence, termination proceeded as scheduled. After notice of termination had been given to depositors, deposits as of that date continue to be insured for two years; any new deposits are uninsured. From 1934 through 1982, the FDIC began only 281 termination proceedings, including 18 in 1982. In about half of these 281 cases the necessary corrections were made, and in most of the others the banks merged or otherwise ceased operations before the termination date was set. In just 15 instances was insurance terminated or banks ceased operations after the date was set.

Cease-and-desist orders have several advantages over insurance termination as enforcement powers. First, they can be aimed at specific infractions. Second, they can be carried out in a more timely fashion, since actual termination of insurance can take more than two years. Third, they provide for involvement of (and therefore review by) the federal courts. Fourth, they can contribute to more safe and sound banking practices without the negative effects that termination proceedings might have. It should be noted, though, that insurance termination remains a viable and sometimes necessary alternative that is still used on occasion. In fact, it remains the FDIC's only significant enforcement power against national and state member banks. The Comptroller of the Currency and the Federal Reserve have cease-and-desist authority over these banks, and generally their supervisory actions protect the interests of the FDIC. As an insurer, though, the FDIC may interpret certain risk situations differently, but the more cumbersome termination proceeding is currently the FDIC's only alternative.[7]

Termination proceedings and cease-and-desist orders are almost always initiated for multiple infractions or problems. While the banking environment might have changed substantially over the years, the unsafe and unsound practices leading to termination proceedings or cease-and-desist orders have changed very little. In 1936, the most frequently cited problems were inadequate capital, excessive insider lending, excessive volume of poor loans, inadequate credit documentation, and incompetent management. In a survey forty years later (1976),

---

[7]Legislation to give the FDIC the full range of enforcement powers over all insured banks is pending in Congress.

these same problems were cited, along with inadequate liquidity and consumer credit law violations.

The Corporation also has the authority to remove or suspend a bank director or officer. This power is infrequently utilized, however, because it can be warranted only by personal dishonesty or willful disregard for the safety and soundness of the bank.

The FDIC also may impose fines on banks or bankers for failure to comply with cease-and-desist orders or with other FDIC rules and regulations. For example, a violation of regulations governing insider lending can result in fines of up to $1,000 per day.

Problem Banks

One of the basic purposes of federal bank examination is to identify banks that pose a greater risk of loss to the federal deposit insurance fund. Banks found to be operating with a deteriorated financial condition, or in a manner likely to lead to such a condition, are subject to more thorough regulatory scrutiny. As has been the case since 1934, the primary supervisory tool is more frequent examination. This affords regulators the best opportunity for verifying the implementation of corrective procedures, measuring their effectiveness and, perhaps most importantly, maintaining communication with management. There are many factors that can cause a bank to be classified as a problem, but over the years the most frequent cause has been poor loan quality, resulting from incompetent or self-serving management.

Prior to 1978, the FDIC used a three-tiered system for problem bank classification.

Serious Problem - Potential Payoff: An advanced serious problem with an estimated 50 percent or more chance of requiring financial assistance by the FDIC.

Serious Problem: A situation that threatens ultimately to involve the FDIC in a financial outlay unless drastic changes occur.

Other Problem: A situation in which a bank has significant weaknesses but the FDIC is less vulnerable. Such banks require aggressive supervision and more than ordinary attention.

In 1978 a new bank rating system was established by the federal supervisory agencies.[8] On the basis of the safety and soundness examination, banks are rated from 1 to 5 in each of five areas: (1) adequacy of capital and reserves, (2) loan and investment quality, (3) management quality, (4) earnings and (5) liquidity. This rating is known by the acronym CAMEL, for Capital, Assets, Management, Earnings and Liquidity. In addition, a bank is given an overall, or composite, rating in the 1 to 5 range. Ratings of 1 or 2 are favorable and represent basic soundness; a 3 rating is marginally unsatisfactory. Ratings of 4 or 5 indicate problem bank status, with a 5 rating designating a high probability of failure.

The FDIC has maintained a confidential list of all insured banks that are considered problem banks. This list is constantly changing, but it generally represents less than four percent of the insured bank population. An analysis of the problem list during a seven-year period in the 1970s revealed these facts about banks in the most serious category:

- 34 percent eventually failed;

- 10 percent were merged into healty organizations without FDIC financial assistance;

- 1 percent received FDIC financial assistance to avert failure; and

- 53 percent improved to a less serious rating or were removed from the problem list altogether.

This system of problem bank identification, coupled with more aggressive supervision of these institutions, has undoubtedly prevented numerous failures. However, many other failures occur in banks not previously identified as problems. In some cases a bank's condition can deteriorate so rapidly that even a 12-month interval between examinations proves too lengthy. Most of the time, these failures relate to fraudulent behavior. Fraud or embezzlement is more difficult to detect at an early stage. In part, this is because bank examinations are not accounting audits; thus, they are not likely to expose accounting-related malfeasance. In the 1940s and 1950s, however, many smaller banks were still not being audited, either internally or externally, on a regular basis, and examiners may have been more attuned to identifying shortages. The FDIC, in

---

[8]The terminology of the rating system was modified slightly in 1980 to accommodate all depository institutions, including thrifts.

128

In W.C. Fields' movie, "The Bank Dick," stalwart bank examiner J. Pinkerton Snoopington overcame numerous diversionary shenanigans by guard Egbert Sousé. "I would go into tse-tse fly country if there were books to be examined," he asserted. Photo: Universal Pictures

fact, had several examiners who were particularly skilled in this area and were utilized as trouble-shooters, traveling to banks around the country that were suspected of improprieties.[9]

In 1977, the FDIC implemented an early warning system to assist in the detection of problem or potential problem banks. The Integrated Monitoring System (IMS), utilizes selected financial ratios from the Reports of Condition and Income as well as examination information in order to identify possible adverse trends in a particular bank or in the industry in general.[10] Its primary use is in monitoring banks between examinations. IMS is computer-based and runs a number of separate tests to determine whether a bank meets minimally acceptable test levels of capital adequacy, liquidity, profitability and asset-liability mix/growth. A bank that "fails" one or more particular test (that is, it does not reach a minimally acceptable level) is referred for further analysis, possibly leading to earlier examination or visitation.

An additional supervisory tool, the uniform bank performance report (UBPR), was developed jointly by the federal bank regulatory agencies in 1982. The report is generated from financial data contained in regularly submitted reports of condition and income and provides a ratio analysis (on a current and trend basis) of an individual bank as well as a percentile ranking for each bank with respect to all banks of a similar size in the same geographic area. These reports, which impose no increased reporting burden, have facilitated the cutback in on-site examinations. In 1983 and 1984, changes in the Report of Condition will provide more detailed asset and liability information, increasing the usefulness of IMS and UBPRs, as well as other analytical systems and tools.

Federal and State Cooperation

Since the FDIC has exercised limited supervisory authority over member banks and shares supervisory responsibility for insured nonmember banks with the banking supervisors of the

---

[9] Interview with John Early (former Director, Division of Bank Supervision), Washington, D.C., August 31, 1983.

[10] Reports of Condition, which are detailed statements of assets, liabilities and capital, are collected quarterly from all insured banks (semi-annually from uninsured banks); Reports of Income, which detail year-to-date income and expenses, are collected quarterly from insured banks.

various states, there is a heavy reliance upon interagency co-operation. FDIC interaction with the other federal bank supervisors began almost with its inception in 1933. In fact, some degree of interagency cooperation was built into the original FDIC structure with the placement of the Comptroller of the Currency on the FDIC's three-person Board of Directors. Standardization among federal agencies was sought and largely established for Reports of Condition and Income, and standardization has been sought for examination forms and procedures. The latter, of course, has been the most difficult to standardize, given the complexities and qualitative nature of so many aspects of the examination process. Interagency conferences were held as early as 1934 to coordinate asset appraisal techniques. While the level of cooperation among the federal agencies has generally been adequate, Congress has occasionally (and perhaps more frequently in recent years) mandated forums to assure agency interaction and coordination.

The 1970s saw the establishment of the Interagency Supervisory Committee, which was superseded by the Federal Financial Institutions Examination Council in 1978. Federal legislation in 1980 created the Depository Institutions Deregulation Committee. All of these organizations have had the task of coordinating the development and application of agency rules and regulations.

National banks hold nearly 60 percent of the deposits in insured commercial banks but have traditionally been outside of the supervisory purview of the FDIC. In December of 1983, the FDIC and the Office of the Comptroller of the Currency entered into an arrangement for the FDIC and the Comptroller to conduct joint examinations of all problem national banks (those with a CAMEL rating of 4 or 5). The FDIC also will join in the examination of a representative sample of nonproblem national banks, including multinational and regional banks and their overseas offices.

The arrangement will greatly enhance the FDIC's ability to assess risks to the insurance fund. Also, because the FDIC will participate in examination-related meetings with national bank management and in meetings at which national bank enforcement actions are determined, the FDIC will have a more active role in helping to control the risks these banks might pose to the fund. Finally, the arrangement will enable FDIC personnel to have earlier access to more detailed information about failing national banks, permitting a more orderly handling of the failures as they occur.

FDIC-state cooperation has been most significant in the area of examination. Because insured state nonmember banks are subject to both federal and state supervision and examination, emphasis has been placed on reducing this dual regulatory burden as much as possible. In 1934, some states accepted copies of FDIC examinations in lieu of performing their own, and other states conducted their examinations jointly with FDIC examiners, sharing the results and greatly reducing any inconvenience to the bank. Some states resented what they viewed as an infringement by a new layer of federal regulation, but in a few instances financial considerations forced their capitulation. Many state banking departments were severely underfunded in 1934. In fact, the state banking departments were sometimes combined with the office of the state insurance regulator so that the bank supervisory functions could be underwritten to some extent by the fees paid by insurance companies.

While there still exists a great deal of variation among the state banking departments and regulatory structures, wherever feasible the FDIC has entered into programs of concurrent, joint or alternating examinations. In 1974, the FDIC entered into a two-year experiment with the states of Georgia, Iowa, and Washington, wherein the FDIC would withdraw from the examination of certain banks and would rely on the state examination reports. It was hoped that the experiment would prove beneficial not only to the banks, in terms of reduced regulatory burden, but also to the FDIC and the states, which might eventually be able to reduce or at least reallocate their resources. The experiment did not include problem banks or others requiring special supervisory attention, nor did it include banks with assets of more than $100 million. Thus, the intent was to devote fewer resources to smaller, non-problem institutions. Following the two-year period, the FDIC examined many of the participating banks and found that, in most instances, the state reports were sufficiently reliable. There are now 27 states participating in the divided examination program, in which the FDIC and the states examine banks during alternate examination cycles, relying on each other's reports in the interim.

Summary

Even before the banking crisis of the 1930s and the establishment of the FDIC, two other federal agencies and each of the states supervised commercial banks even though the pre-1930s environment was characterized by relatively free banking. The FDIC was established to protect depositors, to restore confidence in the banking system and to eliminate most of the secondary consequences of bank failures that had afforded the rationale for bank supervision. The establishment of the FDIC provided an additional rationale for bank supervision, which was monitoring and restricting bank risk to limit the exposure of the insurance system.

When banking stabilized and failures declined, banks remained very cautious as the Depression experience continued to influence bank behavior. Bank supervision contributed to this cautious behavior and, by restricting entry, helped insulate banking from competition. For an extended period following World War II, bank supervisors continued to examine virtually all banks, assess asset exposure and carry out audit-type functions even though few banks posed any potential risk to the insurance fund.

When banks began to become more aggressive and the number and size of bank failures increased, the FDIC began to reallocate resources, reducing examination coverage of better performing banks. Most of the major changes in FDIC examination procedures in the past decade have been oriented toward improved supervision of problem and potential-problem situations. An arrangement entered into in late 1983 calling for joint FDIC/Comptroller examinations of certain national banks reflects this shift in FDIC orientation. The increased use of cease-and-desist powers, the development of a computerized monitoring system and the development of a uniform rating system were all implemented to facilitate the concentration of resources in areas that posed the greatest exposure to the deposit insurance fund. The lengthened examination cycle for favorably rated banks, reduced attention to branch and routine merger approvals and the divided examination program are all areas where the FDIC has reallocated resources from areas where insurance fund exposure is minimal. The FDIC has moved to the position where it considers the principal purpose of bank examinations to be to limit the exposure of the deposit insurance fund.

Epilogue

This history has been written from a 1983 perspective, and the importance given to certain earlier events might have been quite different had this been, for example, a 40-year history written in 1973. In several chapters, discussion has been divided into three periods: the Depression and post-Depression years of the 1930s; the long period of few bank failures and low unemployment running for about 30 years from the onset of World War II; and the past ten years, when banking markets have been more competitive, the economic environment has been more hostile and the number and size of bank failures have increased. These divisions require some convenient simplifications. While the number of bank failures remained high through the early 1940s, many of these resulted from problems encountered much earlier. Banking conditions had actually stabilized as early as the mid-1930s. Also, banking did not suddenly become more competitive and deregulated in 1973; that process was well underway during the 1960s.

The issues and problems faced by the FDIC today are very different from those faced 20 or 25 years ago. Many changes have occurred in the financial services industry in recent years and are continuing. In 1980 and 1982, Congress passed major legislation that has significantly affected banks and financial markets. Congress is currently considering legislation that could substantially alter the activities permitted by banks and thrift institutions and the manner in which they are to be regulated.

In 1983, loan losses at commercial banks were at their highest rate in 40 years and, for the most part, these figures did not include the enormous volume of rescheduled loans in less developed countries. Bank capital ratios, while not materially changed in recent years, were close to their lowest level since anyone started counting. Most thrifts, which have become less distinguishable from commercial banks, were seriously under-capitalized, even if one focused on book values. At the same time, competition has been increased in many areas. As entry barriers are dismantled and many banks and thrifts anticipate selling out to larger institutions, they find their franchise values have diminished.

The number of bank failures in 1983 surpassed that of any year since 1939. Even in an improving economic environment, a more competitive banking system is likely to result in more bank failures than the FDIC was used to up until the past few years.

The FDIC has been very active in the past decade in an environment characterized by two very steep recessions, a high inflation rate and wide swings in interest rates. Failures, for the most part, have been handled smoothly and at modest cost. Confidence in the banking system has been retained.

Some argue that the FDIC has provided too much protection to large depositors, with the result that there has been insufficient depositor discipline. These issues are addressed in the FDIC deposit insurance study, which was published in the spring of 1983. If banking is to be less regulated, then *de facto* insurance coverage probably has to be reduced or some other device — perhaps more private capital — probably needs to cushion the system from loss and restrain excessive risk taking. In November 1983, the FDIC introduced legislation designed to strengthen its position as an insurer. This legislation would enable the FDIC to price insurance more in line with bank risk and would make it easier for the FDIC to pay off rather than merge failed banks, thereby reducing *de facto* insurance coverage.

In 1984, the deposit insurance and supervisory systems will be under active scrutiny. There is a general appreciation that deposit insurance as an institution is very important to our system today — ten years ago that might not have been the case. There is an increasing appreciation that it is insurance that sets depository institutions apart and affords the rationale for federal supervision.

It is not the function of this history to predict how the FDIC will evolve in the future. In periods of adversity or change, the stability provided by the FDIC has tended to gain importance, and as this 50th anniversary passes, the FDIC's importance seems greater than at any time since the 1930s.

Appendix

139

05-10-53 to 04-17-57
Henry E. Cook, Chairman
Maple T. Harl
Ray M. Gidney

04-17-57 to 08-05-57
Henry E. Cook, Chairman
Vacant
Ray M. Gidney

08-05-57 to 09-06-57
Henry E. Cook, Chairman
Erle Cocke, Sr.
Ray M. Gidney

09-06-57 to 09-17-57
Ray M. Gidney, Acting
 Chairman
Erle Cocke, Sr.
Vacant

09-17-57 to 01-20-61
Jesse P. Wolcott, Chairman
Erle Cocke, Sr.
Ray M. Gidney

01-20-61 to 11-15-61
Erle Cocke, Sr., Chairman
Jesse P. Wolcott
Ray M. Gidney

11-15-61 to 08-04-63
Erle Cocke, Sr., Chairman
Jesse P. Wolcott
James J. Saxon

08-04-63 to 01-22-64
James J. Saxon, Acting
 Chairman
Jesse P. Wolcott
Vacant

01-22-64 to 01-26-64
Joseph W. Barr, Chairman
Jesse P. Wolcott
James J. Saxon

01-26-64 to 03-10-64
Joseph W. Barr, Chairman
Vacant
James J. Saxon

03-10-64 to 04-21-65
Joseph W. Barr, Chairman
Kenneth A. Randall
James J. Saxon

04-21-65 to 04-28-65
Kenneth A. Randall, Chairman
Joseph W. Barr
James J. Saxon

04-28-65 to 03-04-66
Kenneth A. Randall, Chairman
Vacant
James J. Saxon

03-04-66 to 11-15-66
Kenneth A. Randall, Chairman
William W. Sherrill
James J. Saxon

11-15-66 to 04-30-67
Kenneth A. Randall, Chairman
William W. Sherrill
William B. Camp

04-30-67 to 09-27-68
Kenneth A. Randall, Chairman
Vacant
William B. Camp

09-27-68 to 03-09-70
Kenneth A. Randall, Chairman
Irvine H. Sprague
William B. Camp

140

03-09-70 to 04-01-70
William B. Camp, Acting
    Chairman
Irvine H. Sprague
Vacant

04-01-70 to 02-15-73
Frank Wille, Chairman
Irvine H. Sprague
William B. Camp

02-15-73 to 03-23-73
Frank Wille, Chairman
Vacant
William B. Camp

03-23-73 to 07-05-73
Frank Wille, Chairman
Vacant
Justin T. Watson, Acting
    Comptroller of the Currency

07-05-73 to 08-01-73
Frank Wille, Chairman
Vacant
James E. Smith

08-01-73 to 03-16-76
Frank Wille, Chairman
George A. LeMaistre
James E. Smith

03-16-76 to 03-18-76
James E. Smith, Acting
    Chairman
George A. LeMaistre
Vacant

03-18-76 to 07-30-76
Robert E. Barnett, Chairman
George A. LeMaistre
James E. Smith

07-30-76 to 06-01-77
Robert E. Barnett, Chairman
George A. LeMaistre
Robert Bloom, Acting
    Comptroller of the Currency

06-01-77 to 07-12-77
George A. LeMaistre,
    Chairman
Vacant
Robert Bloom, Acting
    Comptroller of the Currency

07-12-77 to 03-30-78
George A. LeMaistre,
    Chairman
Vacant
John G. Heimann

03-30-78 to 08-16-78
George A. LeMaistre,
    Chairman
William M. Isaac
John G. Heimann

08-16-78 to 02-07-79
John G. Heimann, Acting
    Chairman
William M. Isaac
Vacant

02-07-79 to 05-15-81
Irvine H. Sprague, Chairman
William M. Isaac
John G. Heimann

05-16-81 to 08-02-81
Irvine H. Sprague, Chairman
William M. Isaac
Charles E. Lord, Acting
    Comptroller of the Currency

08-03-81 to 12-15-81
William M. Isaac, Chairman
Irvine H. Sprague
Charles E. Lord, Acting
  Comptroller of the Currency

12-16-81 to
William M. Isaac, Chairman
Irvine H. Sprague
C. T. Conover

Bibliography

Auerbach, Ronald P. *An Appraisal of Bank Failures in the Great Depression*. Washington, D.C.: Federal Deposit Insurance Corporation, 1979.

"Bank Bill Debate to Open in Senate." *New York Times*, 19 May 1933, p. 4.

"Bankers Meet: Deposit Insurance a Thorn, but They Look to Postal Savings Deposits." *The News-Week in Business*, 16 September 1933.

"Biggest Liquidator of Them All." *Forbes*, 15 February 1977.

Bremer, C. D. *American Bank Failures*. New York: Columbia University Press, 1935.

Burns, Helen M. *The American Banking Community and New Deal Banking Reforms, 1933-1935*. Westport, CT.: Greenwood Press, 1974.

"Deposit Insurance." *Business Week*, 12 April 1933.

"Early Claim Agents Had Key Role in Payoff of Insured Deposits." *FDIC News*, August 1983.

Early, John. Former Director, Division of Bank Supervision, Federal Deposit Insurance Corporation. Washington, D.C. Interview, 31 August 1983.

"FDIC Pioneer Recalls 'Early Days'." *FDIC News*, June 1983.

Federal Deposit Insurance Corporation. *Annual Reports*. Washington, D.C.: Federal Deposit Insurance Corporation, 1934-1982.

Federal Deposit Insurance Corporation. *Deposit Insurance in a Changing Environment*. Washington, D.C.: Federal Deposit Insurance Corporation, 1983.

Friedman, Milton, and Schwartz, Anna J. *A Monetary History of the United States, 1867-1960*. Princeton, New Jersey: National Bureau of Economic Research, 1963.

Golembe, Carter H. *Golembe Reports*. Vol. 1974-8: *Memorandum re: Bank Failures and All That*. Washington, D.C.: Carter H. Golembe Associates, Inc., 1974.

Golembe, Carter H. "Origins of Deposit Insurance in the Middle West, 1834-1866." *The Indiana Magazine of History*, Vol. LI (June 1955).

Golembe, Carter H. "The Deposit Insurance Legislation of 1933: An Examination of Its Antecedents and Its Purposes." *Political Science Quarterly*, Vol. LXXV (June 1960).

Golembe, Carter H., and Warburton, Clark. *Insurance of Bank Obligations in Six States*. Washington, D.C.: Federal Deposit Insurance Corporation, 1958.

Greensides, Neil. Former Chief, Division of Examinations, Federal Deposit Insurance Corporation. Washington, D.C. Interview, 16 August 1983.

Horvitz, Paul M. "Failures of Large Banks: Implications for Banking Supervision and Deposit Insurance." *Journal of Financial and Quantitative Analysis* (November 1975).

Jones, Homer. "Insurance of Bank Deposits in the United States of America." *The Economic Journal*, Vol. XLVIII (December 1938).

Jones, Homer. "Some Problems of Bank Supervision." *Journal of the American Statistical Association*, Vol. 33 (June 1938).

Jones, Jesse H. *Fifty Billion Dollars: My Thirteen Years with the RFC, 1933-1945*. New York: The Macmillan Company, 1951.

Kennedy, Susan Estabrook. *The Banking Crisis of 1933*. Lexington, KY.: University Press of Kentucky, 1973.

Klebaner, Benjamin J. *Commercial Banking in the United States: A History*. Hinsdale, Illinois: The Dryden Press, 1974.

Krooss, Herman E., ed. *Documentary History of Banking and Currency in the United States*, Vol. IV. New York: Chelsea House Publishers, 1969.

Moley, Raymond. *The First New Deal.* New York: Harcourt, Brace & World, Inc., 1966.

New York, General Assembly. *Letter from Joshua Forman.* Assembly Journal, 1829.

Schisgall, Oscar. *Out of One Small Chest.* New York: AMACOM, 1975.

Silverberg, Stanley C. "Implications of Changes in the Effective Level of Deposit Insurance Coverage." *Proceedings of a Conference on Bank Structure and Competition.* Chicago, Ill.: Federal Reserve Bank of Chicago, 1980.

Sinkey, Joseph F., Jr. "Problem and Failed Institutions in the Commercial Banking Industry." *Contemporary Studies in Economic and Financial Analysis*, Vol. 4. Greenwich, CT.: JAI Press, Inc., 1979.

"The Cabinet." *Time*, 20 March 1933.

U.S. Comptroller of the Currency. *Annual Reports.* Washington, D.C.: Government Printing Office, 1864, 1895, 1933.

U.S. Congress. House. Committee on Banking and Currency. *Hearings before the House Committee on Banking and Currency on H.R. (10241) 11362*, 72d Cong., 1st sess., 1932.

U.S. Congress. House. Committee on Banking and Currency. *Hearings before the House Committee on Banking and Currency on S. 3025*, 73rd Cong., 2d sess., 1934.

U.S. Congress. House. Dedication of the Federal Deposit Insurance Corporation Building. 88th Cong., 1st sess., 18 June 1963. *Congressional Record*, Vol. 109, part 8.

U.S. Congress. Senate. Committee on Banking and Currency. *Hearings before a subcommittee of the Senate Committee on Banking and Currency on Bills to Amend the Federal Deposit Insurance Act*, 81st Cong., 2d sess., 1950.

U.S. Congress. Senate. Committee on Banking and Currency. *Hearings before a subcommittee of the Senate Committee on Banking and Currency on the Nominations of H. Earl Cook and Maple T. Harl to be Members of the Board of Directors of the Federal Deposit Insurance Corporation*, 82d Cong., 1st sess., 1951.

Vedder, Richard Kent. "History of the Federal Deposit Insurance Corporation, 1934-1964." Ph.D. dissertation, University of Illinois, 1965.

Warburton, Clark. *Deposit Insurance in Eight States During the Period 1908-1930*. Washington, D.C.: Federal Deposit Insurance Corporation, 1959.

Upham, Cyril B., and Lamke, Edwin. *Closed and Distressed Banks — A Study in Public Administration*. Washington, D.C.: The Brookings Institution, 1934.